Vademec

A Pilgrim's Handbook

Compiled by Joseph Shaw

Latin Mass Society

Cover photograph: *Latin Mass Society Pilgrims on the road to Walsingham, 26/08/17,* by John Aron (www.johnaronphotography.co.uk)

Imprimatur + VINCENT CARD. NICHOLS (Archbishop of Westminster)

Nihil Obstat TERRY TASTARD (Censor)
Date: 18 November 2017

The Latin Mass Society
11-13 Macklin Street
London WC2B 5NH
www.lms.org.uk

ISBN: 978-0-244-66631-6

Printed by Lulu

So now, my brethren, let us sing, not to delight our leisure, but to ease our toil. In the way that travellers are in the habit of singing, sing, but keep on walking. What does it mean, "keep on walking"? Go onward always—but go onward in goodness, for there are, according to the Apostle, some people who go ever onward from bad to worse. If you are going onward, you are walking; but always go onward in goodness, onward in the right faith, onward in good habits and behaviour. Sing, and walk onwards.

St. Augustine (Sermo 256, I.2.3.: PL 38, 1191-1193)

When England returns to Walsingham, Our Lady will return to England.

Pope Leo XIII

Vademecum Peregrini:
The LMS Pilgrim's Handbook

In this Handbook we have attempted to include as much as possible which is helpful to pilgrims on the Walsingham, and other, pilgrimages. In addition to the Ordinary of the Mass, and a range of chants, hymns, and songs for the walking pilgrim, we have included a selection of prayers and devotions, and the Mass propers used on a number of pilgrimages. In many places we have used the texts (and adopted the capitalisations) of the *Manual of Prayers* authorised by the Bishops of England and Wales in 1953.

The Ordinary of the Mass is designed to make possible assistance at Low, Sung, High and Pontifical Mass. Elements of the Mass Ordinary not always used—Gloria, Creed, and blessings included only in Pontifical Mass— are indented and printed in smaller type.

We should like to thank Thomas Windsor (the Society of St Bede) and Francis Bevan for re-setting the chant notation and modern notation, respectively, of many chants, hymns, and other songs.

The translation of the Mass Ordinary, which corresponds to that used in the Latin Mass Society's booklet *The Ordinary Prayers of the Traditional Latin Mass,* is by RPD.

We are grateful to Colin Mawby, a Patron of the LMS, for composing music for the *Song of the English Zouaves*, and allowing us to reproduce it.

We are grateful to Fr Bede Rowe for permission to reproduce his setting of the *Hail Mary*.

We are also very grateful for permission from Richard Connolly, the composer, to reproduce his music for the hymn *Help of Christians;* and for permission to reproduce the words, by the late James McAuly:

By Arrangement with the Licensor, The James McAuley Estate, c/- Curtis Brown (Aust) Pty Ltd.

Contents

PART I: LITURGY

ORDO MISSÆ

Initium Missæ

Sacerdos: In nómine Patris, ✠ et Fílii, et Spíritus Sancti. Amen.

Introíbo ad altáre Dei.

Ministri: Ad Deum, qui lætíficat iuventútem meam.

S: Iúdica me, Deus, et discérne causam meam de gente non sancta: ab hómine iníquo et dolóso érue me.

M: Quia tu es, Deus, fortitúdo mea: quare me repulísti, et quare tristis incédo, dum afflígit me inimícus?

S: Emítte lucem tuam et veritátem tuam: ipsa me deduxérunt, et adduxérunt in montem sanctum tuum, et in tabernácula tua.

M: Et introíbo ad altáre Dei: ad Deum, qui lætíficat iuventútem meam.

S: Confitébor tibi in cíthara, Deus, Deus meus: quare tristis es, ánima mea, et quare contúrbas me?

M: Spera in Deo, quóniam adhuc confitébor illi: salutáre vultus mei, et Deus meus.

S: Glória Patri, et Fílio, et Spirítui Sancto.

M: Sicut erat in princípio, et nunc, et semper: et in sǽcula sæculórum. Amen.

S: Introíbo ad altáre Dei.

M: Ad Deum, qui lætíficat iuventútem meam.

S: Adiutórium nostrum ✠ in nómine Dómini.

M: Qui fecit cælum et terram.

S: Confíteor Deo omnipoténti, beátæ Maríæ semper Vírgini, beáto Michaéli Archángelo, beáto Ioánni Baptístæ, sanctis Apóstolis Petro et Paulo, omnibus Sanctis, et vobis, fratres, quia peccávi nimis cogitatióne, verbo et ópere: mea culpa, mea culpa, mea máxima culpa. Ideo

THE ORDINARY OF THE MASS

Prayers at the Foot of the Altar

Priest: In the name of the Father, ✠ and of the Son, and of the Holy Ghost. Amen.
I will go in to the altar of God.
Ministers: To God who gives joy to my youth.
P: Judge me, O God, and distinguish my cause from the nation that is not holy: deliver me from the unjust and deceitful man.
M: For thou, O God, art my strength: why hast thou cast me off? and why do I go sorrowful whilst the enemy afflicts me?
P: Send forth thy light and thy truth: they have conducted me and brought me unto thy holy hill, even into thy tabernacles.
M: And I will go in to the altar of God, to God, who gives joy to my youth.
P: To thee, O God my God, I will give praise upon the harp: why art thou sad, O my soul? and why dost thou disquiet me?
M: Hope in God, for I will still give praise to him: the salvation of my countenance, and my God.
P: Glory be to the Father and to the Son and to the Holy Ghost.
M: As it was in the beginning, is now and ever shall be, world without end. Amen.
P: I will go in to the altar of God.
M: To God who gives joy to my youth.
P: Our help ✠ is in the name of the Lord
M: Who made heaven and earth.

P: I confess to almighty God, to blessed Mary ever-Virgin, to blessed Michael the Archangel, to blessed John the Baptist, to the holy Apostles Peter and Paul, to all the Saints, and to you, brothers, that I have sinned exceedingly in thought, word and deed, through my fault, through

precor beátam Maríam semper Vírginem, beátum Michaélem Archángelum, beátum Ioánnem Baptístam, sanctos Apóstolos Petrum et Paulum, omnes Sanctos, et vos, fratres, oráre pro me ad Dóminum, Deum nostrum.

M: Misereátur tui omnipotens Deus, et, dimíssis peccátis tuis, perdúcat te ad vitam ætérnam.

S: Amen.

M: Confíteor Deo omnipoténti, beátæ Maríæ semper Vírgini, beáto Michaéli Archángelo, beáto Ioánni Baptístæ, sanctis Apóstolis Petro et Paulo, omnibus Sanctis, et tibi, Pater, quia peccávi nimis cogitatióne, verbo et ópere: mea culpa, mea culpa, mea máxima culpa. Ideo precor beátam Maríam semper Vírginem, beátum Michaélem Archángelum, beátum Ioánnem Baptístam, sanctos Apóstolos Petrum et Paulum, omnes Sanctos, et te, Pater, oráre pro me ad Dóminum, Deum nostrum.

S: Misereátur vestri omnípotens Deus, et, dimíssis peccátis vestris, perdúcat vos ad vitam ætérnam.

M: Amen.

S: Indulgéntiam, ✠ absolutiónem, et remissiónem peccatórum nostrórum tríbuat nobis omnípotens et miséricors Dóminus.

M: Amen.

S: Deus, tu convérsus vivificábis nos.

M: Et plebs tua lætábitur in te.

S: Osténde nobis, Dómine, misericórdiam tuam.

M: Et salutáre tuum da nobis.

S: Dómine, exáudi oratiónem meam.

M: Et clamor meus ad te véniat.

S: Dóminus vobíscum

M: Et cum spíritu tuo.

S: Orémus. Aufer a nobis, quǽsumus, Dómine, iniquitátes nostras: ut ad Sancta sanctórum puris mereámur méntibus introíre. Per Christum Dóminum nostrum. Amen.

Oramus te, Dómine, per mérita Sanctórum tuórum, quorum relíquiæ hic sunt, et ómnium Sanctórum: ut indulgére dignéris ómnia peccáta mea. Amen.

my fault, through my most grievous fault. Therefore I beseech blessed Mary ever-Virgin, blessed Michael the Archangel, blessed John the Baptist, the holy Apostles Peter and Paul, all the saints, and you, brothers, to pray for me to the Lord our God.

M: May almighty God have mercy on thee, and lead thee, with thy sins forgiven, to eternal life.

P: Amen.

M: I confess to almighty God, to blessed Mary ever-Virgin, to blessed Michael the Archangel, to blessed John the Baptist, to the holy Apostles Peter and Paul, to all the Saints, and to thee, Father, that I have sinned exceedingly in thought, word and deed, through my fault, through my fault, through my most grievous fault. Therefore I beseech blessed Mary ever-Virgin, blessed Michael the archangel, blessed John the Baptist, the holy apostles Peter and Paul, all the saints, and thee, Father, to pray for me to the Lord our God.

P: May almighty God have mercy on you, and lead you, with your sins forgiven, to eternal life.

M: Amen.

P: May the almighty and merciful Lord grant us pardon, ✠ absolution and remission of our sins.

M: Amen.

P: Thou wilt turn, O God, and bring us to life.

M: And thy people shall rejoice in thee.

P: Show us, O Lord, thy mercy.

M: And grant us thy salvation.

P: O Lord, hear my prayer.

M: And let my cry come unto thee.

P: The Lord be with you.

M: And with thy spirit.

P: Let us pray. Take away from us our iniquities, we pray, O Lord, that with pure minds we may worthily go in to the holy of holies. Through Christ our Lord. Amen. We beseech thee, O Lord, by the merits of thy saints, whose relics are here, and of all the saints, that thou wouldst be pleased to forgive me all my sins. Amen.

11

At High Mass:
S: Ab illo benedicáris, in cuius honóre cremáberis. Amen.

MISSA CATECHUMENORUM

Introit: see Propers

S: Kyrie, eléison.
M: Kyrie, eléison.
S: Kyrie, eléison.
M: Christe, eléison.
S: Christe, eléison.
M: Christe, eléison.
S: Kyrie, eléison.
M: Kyrie, eléison.
S: Kyrie, eléison.

S: Gloria in excélsis Deo.
S/Chorus: Et in terra pax homínibus bonæ voluntátis. Laudámus te. Benedícimus te. Adorámus te. Glorificámus te. Grátias ágimus tibi propter magnam glóriam tuam. Dómine Deus, Rex cæléstis, Deus Pater omnípotens.
  Dómine Fili unigénite, Iesu Christe. Dómine Deus, Agnus Dei, Fílius Patris. Qui tollis peccáta mundi, miserére nobis. Qui tollis peccáta mundi, súscipe deprecatiónem nostram. Qui sedes ad déxteram Patris, miserére nobis. Quóniam tu solus Sanctus. Tu solus Dóminus. Tu solus Altíssimus, Iesu Christe.
  Cum Sancto Spiritu ✠ in gloria Dei Patris. Amen.

S: Dóminus vobíscum.
M: Et cum spíritu tuo.
S: Oremus.

Collect: see Propers

M: Amen

Epistle: see Propers

M: Deo grátias.

At High Mass:
P: Be thou blessed by him in whose honour thou shalt be
burned. Amen.

MASS OF CATECHUMENS

P: Lord, have mercy.

M: Lord, have mercy.

P: Lord, have mercy.

M: Christ, have mercy.

P: Christ, have mercy.

M: Christ, have mercy.

P: Lord, have mercy.

M: Lord, have mercy.

P: Lord, have mercy.

P: Glory to God in the highest,

P/Choir: And on earth peace to men of good will. We
praise thee. We bless thee. We adore thee. We glorify
thee. We give thee thanks for thy great glory. Lord God,
heavenly King, O God almighty Father.

Lord Jesus Christ, Only Begotten Son. Lord God,
Lamb of God, Son of the Father; who takest away the
sins of the world, have mercy on us; who takest away
the sins of the world, receive our prayer; who sittest at
the right hand of the Father, have mercy on us. For thou
alone art the Holy One. thou alone art the Lord. Thou
alone art the Most High, Jesus Christ,

With the Holy Ghost, ✠ in the glory of God the Father. Amen.

P: The Lord be with you.

R: And with thy spirit.

P: Let us pray.

M: Amen.

M: Thanks be to God.

Gradual, Alleluia, &c.: see Propers

S/Diaconus: Munda cor meum, ac lábia mea, omnípotens Deus, qui lábia Isaíæ prophétæ cálculo mundásti igníto: ita me tua grata miseratióne dignáre mundáre, ut sanctum Evangélium tuum digne váleam nuntiáre. Per Christum Dóminum nostrum. Amen.

S/D: Iube, domne (*vel* Dómine), benedícere.

P: Dóminus sit in corde tuo (meo) et in lábiis tuis (meis): ut digne et competénter annúnties (annúntiem) Evangélium suum.

> *At High Mass:*
> In nómine Patris, et Fílii, ✠ et Spíritus Sancti.
> Amen.

S/D: Dóminus vobíscum.

M: Et cum spíritu tuo.

S/D: Inítium (*vel* Sequéntia) sancti Evangélii secúndum N...

M: Glória tibi, Dómine.

Gospel: see Propers

M: Laus tibi, Christe.

S: Per evangélica dicta deleántur nostra delícta.

Sermon, when preached

S: Credo in unum Deum.

S/Chorus: Patrem omnipoténtem, factórem cæli et terræ, visibílium ómnium et invisibílium.

Et in unum Dóminum Iesum Christum, Fílium Dei unigénitum. Et ex Patre natum ante ómnia sǽcula. Deum de Deo, lumen de lúmine, Deum verum de Deo vero. Génitum, non factum, consubstantiálem Patri: per quem ómnia facta sunt. Qui propter nos hómines et propter nostram salútem descéndit de cælis. **Et incarnatus est de Spiritu Sancto ex Maria Virgine: Et homo factus**

P/Deacon. Cleanse my heart and my lips, almighty God, who didst cleanse the lips of the prophet Isaias with a burning coal: be pleased by thy gracious mercy so to cleanse me that I may worthily proclaim thy holy Gospel. Through Christ our Lord. Amen.

P/D: Pray, sir (*or* Lord), a blessing.

P: May the Lord be in thy (my) heart and on thy (my) lips, that thou mayst (I may) proclaim his Gospel worthily and well.

> *At High Mass:*
> In the name of the Father, and of the Son, ✠ and of the Holy Ghost. Amen.

P/D: The Lord be with you.

M: And with thy spirit.

P/D: The beginning (*or* continuation) of the holy Gospel according to N...

M: Glory to thee, O Lord.

M: Praise to thee, O Christ.

P: Through the words of the Gospel may our sins be wiped away.

> *P:* I believe in one God.
> *P/Choir:* the Father almighty, maker of heaven and earth, of all things visible and invisible.
>   And in one Lord Jesus Christ, the Son of God, only begotten, and born of the Father before all ages.
> God from God, light from light, true God from true God, begotten, not made, consubstantial with the Father; through him all things were made. For us men and for our salvation he came down from heaven, **and was incarnate by the Holy Ghost from the Virgin Mary,**

est. Crucifíxus étiam pro nobis: sub Póntio Piláto passus, et sepúltus est. Et resurréxit tértia die, secúndum Scriptúras. Et ascéndit in cælum, sedet ad déxteram Patris. Et íterum ventúrus est cum glória iudicáre vivos et mórtuos: cujus regni non erit finis.

Et in Spíritum Sanctum, Dóminum et vivificántem: qui ex Patre Filióque procédit. Qui cum Patre et Fílio simul adorátur et conglorificátur: qui locútus est per Prophétas.

Et unam, sanctam, cathólicam et apostólicam Ecclésiam. Confiteor unum baptísma in remissiónem peccatórum. Et exspécto resurrectiónem mortuórum.

Et vitam ✠ ventúri sǽculi. Amen.

S: Dóminus vobíscum.
M: Et cum spíritu tuo.
S: Orémus.

MISSA FIDELIUM

Offertorium

Offertory: see Propers

S: Súscipe, sancte Pater, omnípotens ætérne Deus, hanc immaculátam hóstiam, quam ego indígnus fámulus tuus óffero tibi Deo meo vivo et vero, pro innumerabílibus peccátis, et offensiónibus, et neglegéntiis meis, et pro ómnibus circumstántibus, sed et pro ómnibus fidélibus christiánis vivis atque defúnctis: ut mihi, et illis profíciat ad salútem in vitam ætérnam. Amen.

Deus, qui humánæ substántiæ dignitátem mirabíliter condidísti, et mirabílius reformásti: da nobis per huius aquæ et vini mystérium, eius divinitátis esse consórtes, qui humanitátis nostræ fíeri dignátus est párticeps, Iesus Christus, Fílius tuus, Dóminus noster: Qui tecum vivit et regnat in unitáte Spíritus Sancti, Deus, per ómnia sǽcula sæculórum. Amen.

and was made man. He was crucified also for us under Pontius Pilate, he suffered and was buried, and rose again on the third day in accordance with the Scriptures. And ascended into heaven, and is seated at the right hand of the Father. And he will come again with glory to judge the living and the dead: and his kingdom will have no end.

And in the Holy Ghost, the Lord, the giver of life, who proceeds from the Father and the Son, who together with the Father and the Son is adored and glorified, who has spoken through the Prophets.

And one, holy, catholic and apostolic Church. I confess one baptism for the forgiveness of sins. And I look forward to the resurrection of the dead. And the life ✠ of the world to come. Amen.

P: The Lord be with you.
M: And with thy spirit.
P: Let us pray.

MASS OF THE FAITHFUL
Offertory

P: Receive, O holy Father, almighty and everlasting God, this spotless Victim, which I, thy unworthy servant, offer unto thee, my living and true God, for my numberless sins, offences, and negligences; and for all here present; as also for all faithful Christians living and dead, that it may avail for their salvation and mine, unto life everlasting. Amen.

O God, who wondrously didst create the dignity of human nature and still more wondrously hast restored it: grant that, by the mystery of this water and wine, we may come to share in the divinity of him who humbled himself to share in our humanity, Jesus Christ thy Son, our Lord: who lives and reigns with thee in the unity of the Holy Ghost, one God, for ever and ever. Amen.

17

Offérimus tibi, Dómine, cálicem salutáris, tuam depre-
cántes cleméntiam: ut in conspéctu divínæ maiestátis tuæ,
pro nostra et totíus mundi salúte cum odóre suavitátis
ascéndat. Amen.

In spíritu humilitátis et in ánimo contríto suscipiámur a te,
Dómine: et sic fiat sacrifícium nostrum in conspéctu tuo
hódie, ut pláceat tibi, Dómine Deus.

Veni, sanctificátor omnípotens, ætérne Deus: et bénedic ✠
hoc sacrifícium tuo sancto nómini præparátum.

> *At High Mass*
> Per intercessiónem beáti Michaélis Archángeli, stantis a
> dextris altáris incénsi, et ómnium electórum suórum,
> incénsum istud dignétur Dóminus benedícere ✠ et in
> odórem suavitátis accípere. Per Christum Dóminum
> nostrum. Amen.
>
> Incensum istud a te benedíctum, ascéndat ad te,
> Dómine: et descéndat super nos misericórdia tua.
>
> Dirigatur, Dómine, orátio mea, sicut incénsum in
> conspéctu tuo: elevátio mánuum meárum sacrificium
> vespertínum. Pone, Dómine, custódiam ori meo, et
> óstium circumstántiæ lábiis meis: Ut non declínet cor
> meum in verba malítiæ, ad excusándas excusatiónes in
> peccátis.
>
> Accendat in nobis Dóminus ignem sui amóris, et
> flammam ætérnæ caritátis. Amen.

S: Lavábo inter innocéntes manus meas: et circúmdabo
altáre tuum, Dómine: Ut áudiam vocem laudis, et enárrem
univérsa mirabília tua. Dómine, diléxi decórem domus
tuæ, et locum habitatiónis glóriæ tuæ. Ne perdas cum
ímpiis, Deus, ánimam meam, et cum viris sánguinum
vitam meam: In quorum mánibus iniquitátes sunt: déxtera
eórum repléta est munéribus.

Ego autem in innocéntia mea ingréssus sum: rédime me,
et miserére mei. Pes meus stetit in dirécto: in ecclésiis
benedícam te, Dómine. Glória Patri.

S: Súscipe, sancta Trínitas, hanc oblatiónem, quam tibi
offérimus ob memóriam passiónis, resurrectiónis et as-

We offer unto thee, O Lord, the chalice of salvation, entreating thy clemency, that it may ascend in the sight of thy divine majesty with an odour of sweetness, for our salvation and for that of the whole world. Amen.

With humble spirit and contrite heart may we be accepted by thee, O Lord, and may our sacrifice in thy sight this day be pleasing to thee, Lord God.

Come, O Sanctifier, almighty and eternal God, and bless ✠ this sacrifice made ready for thy holy name.

> *At High Mass*
> Through the intercession of blessed Michael the Archangel standing at the right hand of the altar of incense, and of all his elect, may the Lord be pleased to bless ✠ this incense, and to receive it in the odour of sweetness. Through Christ Our Lord. Amen.
>
> May this incense which thou hast blessed, O Lord, ascend to thee, and may thy mercy descend upon us.
>
> Let my prayer, O Lord, be directed as incense in thy sight; the lifting up of my hands as an evening sacrifice. Set a watch, O Lord, before my mouth, and a door round about my lips: That my heart may not incline to evil words, and seek excuses in sins.
>
> May the Lord kindle within us the fire of his love, and the flame of everlasting charity. Amen.

P: I will wash my hands among the innocent: and will compass thy altar, O Lord. That I may hear the voice of thy praise, and tell of all thy wondrous works. I have loved, O Lord, the beauty of thy house, and the place where thy glory dwells. Take not away my soul, O God, with the wicked, nor my life with bloody men: in whose hands are iniquities: their right hand is filled with gifts. But as for me, I have walked in my innocence: redeem me, and have mercy on me. My foot has stood in the direct way: in the churches I will bless thee, O Lord. Glory be to the Father.

P: Receive, O Holy Trinity, this oblation which we offer unto thee in memory of the passion, resurrection and as-

censiónis Iesu Christi, Dómini nostri: et in honórem beátæ Maríæ semper Vírginis, et beáti Ioánnis Baptístæ, et sanctórum Apostolórum Petri et Pauli, et istórum, et ómnium Sanctórum: ut illis profíciat ad honórem, nobis autem ad salútem: et illi pro nobis intercédere dignéntur in cælis, quorum memóriam ágimus in terris. Per eúndem Christum Dóminum nostrum. Amen.

S: Orate, fratres: ut meum ac vestrum sacrifícium acceptábile fiat apud Deum Patrem omnipoténtem.

M: Suscípiat Dóminus sacrifícium de mánibus tuis, ad laudem et glóriam nóminis sui, ad utilitátem quoque nostram, totiúsque Ecclésiæ suæ sanctæ.

S: Amen.

Secret: see Propers

S: **..per ómnia sǽcula sæculórum.**

M: Amen.

S: Dóminus vobíscum.

M: Et cum spíritu tuo.

S: Sursum corda.

M: Habémus ad Dóminum.

S: Grátias agámus Dómino Deo nostro.

M: Dignum et iustum est.

Præfatio

S: Vere dignum et iustum est, æquum et salutáre, nos tibi semper, et ubíque grátias ágere: Dómine, sancte Pater, omnípotens, ætérne Deus: per Christum Dóminum nostrum. Per quem maiestátem tuam laudant Angeli, adórant Dominatiónes, tremunt Potestátes. Cæli cælorúmque Virtútes ac beáta Séraphim sócia exsultatióne concélebrant. Cum quibus et nostras voces, ut admítti, iúbeas, deprecámur, súpplici conféssióne dicéntes:

Sanctus, Sanctus, Sanctus, Dóminus, Deus Sábaoth.
Pleni sunt cæli et terra glória tua. Hosánna in excélsis.
Benedíctus, qui venit in nómine Dómini. Hosánna in excélsis.

cension of our Lord Jesus Christ, and in honour of blessed Mary ever-Virgin, of blessed John the Baptist, of the holy Apostles Peter and Paul, of these, and of all the saints: that it may avail them for honour and us for salvation: and that they may be pleased to intercede for us in heaven whose commemoration we make on earth. Through the same Christ our Lord. Amen.

P: Pray, brethren, that my sacrifice and yours may be acceptable to God the almighty Father.

M: May the Lord accept the sacrifice at thy hands, for the praise and glory of his name, for our good and the good of all his holy Church.

P: Amen.

P: **...for ever and ever.**

M: Amen.

P: The Lord be with you.

M: And with thy spirit.

P: Lift up your hearts.

M: We lift them up to the Lord.

P: Let us give thanks to the Lord our God.

M: It is right and just.

Preface (the Ordinary Preface: for others, see pp40-1)

P: It is truly right and just, our duty and our salvation, always and everywhere to give thee thanks, Lord, holy Father, almighty and eternal God: through Christ our Lord. Through him the Angels praise your majesty, Dominions adore and Powers tremble before you. Heaven and the Virtues of heaven and the blessed Seraphim worship together in exultation. May our voices, we pray, join with theirs in humble praise as we acclaim:

Holy, Holy, Holy, Lord God of hosts. Heaven and earth are full of thy glory. Hosanna in the highest. Blessed is he who comes in the name of the Lord. Hosanna in the highest.

Canon Missæ

Te ígitur, clementíssime Pater, per Iesum Christum, Fílium tuum, Dóminum nostrum, súpplices rogámus, ac pétimus, uti accépta hábeas et benedícas, hæc ✠ dona, hæc ✠ múnera, hæc ✠ sancta sacrífica illibáta, in primis, quæ tibi offérimus pro Ecclésia tua sancta cathólica: quam pacificáre, custodíre, adunáre, et régere dignéris toto orbe terrárum: una cum fámulo tuo Papa nostro N., et Antístite nostro N., et ómnibus orthodóxis atque cathólicæ et apostólicæ fídei cultóribus.

Memento, Dómine, famulórum famularúmque tuárum N. et N. et ómnium circumstántium, quorum tibi fides cogníta est, et nota devótio, pro quibus tibi offérimus: vel qui tibi ófferunt hoc sacrificium laudis, pro se suísque ómnibus: pro redemptióne animárum suárum, pro spe salútis et incolumitátis suæ: tibíque reddunt vota sua ætérno Deo, vivo et vero.

Communicaántes, et memóriam venerántes, in primis gloriósæ semper Vírginis Maríæ, Genetrícis Dei et Dómini nostri Iesu Christi: sed et beati Ioseph eiusdem Vírginis Sponsi, et beatórum Apostolórum ac Mártyrum tuórum, Petri et Pauli, Andréæ, Iacóbi, Ioánnis, Thomæ, Iacóbi, Philíppi, Bartholomǽi, Matthǽi, Simónis et Thaddǽi, Lini, Cleti, Cleméntis, Xysti, Cornélii, Cypriáni, Lauréntii, Chrysógoni, Ioánnis et Pauli, Cosmæ et Damiáni, et ómnium Sanctórum tuórum; quorum méritis precibúsque concédas, ut in ómnibus protectiónis tuæ muniámur auxílio. Per eúndem Christum Dóminum nostrum. Amen.

Hanc ígitur oblatiónem servitútis nostræ, sed et cunctæ famíliæ tuæ, quǽsumus, Dómine, ut placátus accípias: diésque nostros in tua pace dispónas, atque ab ætérna damnatióne nos éripi, et in electórum tuórum iúbeas grege numerári. Per Christum Dóminum nostrum. Amen.

The Canon of the Mass

To thee, therefore, most merciful Father, we make humble prayer and petition through Jesus Christ, thy Son, our Lord: that thou accept and bless these ✠ gifts, these ✠ offerings, these ✠ holy and unblemished sacrifices, which we offer thee first of all for thy holy catholic Church. Be pleased to grant her peace, to guard, unite and govern her throughout the whole world, together with thy servant N. our Pope and N. our Bishop, and all those who, holding to the truth, hand on the catholic and apostolic faith.

Remember, Lord, thy servants and handmaids N. and N. and all gathered here, whose faith and devotion are known to thee. For them we offer thee this sacrifice of praise, or they offer it for themselves and all who are dear to them, for the redemption of their souls, in hope of health and well-being, and fulfilling their vows to thee, the eternal God, living and true.

In communion with those whose memory we venerate, especially the glorious ever-Virgin Mary, Mother of our God and Lord Jesus Christ, and blessed Joseph, Spouse of the same Virgin, and thy blessed Apostles and Martyrs Peter and Paul, Andrew, James, John, Thomas, James, Philip, Bartholomew, Matthew, Simon and Thaddeus, Linus, Cletus, Clement, Xystus, Cornelius, Cyprian, Lawrence, Chrysogonus, John and Paul, Cosmas and Damian and all thy Saints; through their merits and prayers grant that in all things we may be defended by thy protecting help. Through the same Christ our Lord. Amen.

Therefore, Lord, we pray: graciously accept this oblation of our service, that of your whole family: order our days in thy peace, and command that we be delivered from eternal damnation and counted among the flock of those thou hast chosen. Through Christ our Lord. Amen.

Quam oblatiónem tu, Deus, in ómnibus, quǽsumus, bene-
díctam ✠, adscríptam ✠, ratam ✠, rationábilem, accepta-
bilémque fácere dignéris: ut nobis Corpus ✠,et Sanguis ✠
fiat dilectíssimi Fílii tui Dómini nostri Iesu Christi.

Qui prídie quam paterétur, accépit panem in sanctas ac
venerábiles manus suas, et elevátis óculis in cælum ad te
Deum, Patrem suum omnipoténtem, tibi grátias agens,
benedíxit ✠, fregit, dedítque discípulis suis, dicens:
Accípite, et manducáte ex hoc omnes.

HOC EST ENIM CORPUS MEUM.

Símili modo postquam cenátum est, accípiens et hunc
præclárum Cálicem in sanctas ac venerábiles manus suas:
item tibi grátias agens, benedíxit ✠, dedítque discípulis
suis, dicens: Accípite, et bíbite ex eo omnes.

HIC EST ENIM CALIX SANGUINIS MEI, NOVI ET
ÆTERNI TESTAMENTI: MYSTERIUM FIDEI: QUI
PRO VOBIS ET PRO MULTIS EFFUNDETUR IN RE-
MISSIONEM PECCATORUM.

Hæc quotiescúmque fecéritis, in mei memóriam faciétis.

Unde et mémores, Dómine, nos servi tui, sed et plebs tua
sancta, eiúsdem Christi Fílii tui, Dómini nostri, tam beátæ
passiónis, nec non et ab ínferis resurrectiónis, sed et in
cælos gloriósæ ascensiónis : offérimus præcláræ maiestáti
tuæ, de tuis donis ac datis, hóstiam ✠ puram, hóstiam ✠
sanctam, hóstiam ✠ immaculátam, Panem ✠ sanctum
vitæ ætérnæ, et Cálicem ✠ salútis perpétuæ.

Supra quæ propítio ac seréno vultu respícere dignéris: et

Be pleased, O God, we pray, to bless ✠, acknowledge ✠, and approve ✠ this offering in every respect; make it spiritual and acceptable, so that it may become for us the Body ✠ and Blood ✠ of thy most beloved Son, our Lord Jesus Christ.

On the day before he was to suffer, he took bread in his holy and venerable hands, and with eyes raised to heaven to thee, O God, his almighty Father, giving thanks to thee, he blessed,✠ broke the bread and gave it to his disciples, saying: Take this, all of you, and eat of it,

FOR THIS IS MY BODY.

Likewise, when supper was ended, he took this precious chalice in his holy and venerable hands, and once more giving thanks to thee, he blessed,✠ and gave the chalice to his disciples, saying: Take this, all of you, and drink from it,

FOR THIS IS THE CHALICE OF MY BLOOD, THE BLOOD OF THE NEW AND ETERNAL COVENANT: THE MYSTERY OF FAITH: WHICH WILL BE POURED OUT FOR YOU AND FOR MANY FOR THE FORGIVENESS OF SINS.

As often as ye shall do these things, ye shall do them in memory of me.

Therefore, O Lord, as we celebrate the memorial of the blessed Passion, of the Resurrection from the dead, and the glorious Ascension into heaven of Christ, thy Son, our Lord, we thy servants and thy holy people, offer to thy glorious majesty from the gifts that thou hast given us, this pure ✠ victim, this holy ✠ victim, this spotless ✠ victim, the holy ✠ Bread of eternal life, and the Chalice ✠ of everlasting salvation.

Be pleased to look upon them with serene and kindly

accépta habére, sicúti accépta habére dignátus es múnera
púeri tui iusti Abel, et sacrifícium patriárchæ nostri
Abrahæ: et quod tibi óbtulit summus sacérdos tuus Mel-
chísedech, sanctum sacrifícium, immaculátam hóstiam.

Súpplices te rogámus, omnípotens Deus: iube hæc perfé-
rri per manus sancti Angeli tui in sublíme altáre tuum, in
conspéctu divínæ maiestátis tuæ: ut quotquot ex hac
altáris participatióne sacrosánctum Fílii tui Corpus ✠ et
Sánguinem ✠ sumpsérimus, omni benedictióne cælésti et
grátia repleámur. Per eúndem Christum Dóminum nostrum. Amen.

Meménto étiam, Dómine, famulórum, famularúmque
tuárum N. et N. qui nos præcessérunt cum signo fídei, et
dórmiunt in somno pacis.

Ipsis, Dómine, et ómnibus in Christo quiescéntibus locum
refrigérii, lucis et pacis, ut indúlgeas, deprecámur. Per
eúndem Christum Dóminum nostrum. Amen.

Nobis quoque peccatóribus fámulis tuis, de multitúdine
miseratiónum tuárum sperántibus, partem áliquam, et
societátem donáre dignéris, cum tuis sanctis Apóstolis et
Martyribus: cum Ioánne, Stéphano, Matthía, Bárnaba,
Ignátio, Alexándro, Marcellíno, Petro, Felicitáte,
Perpétua, Agatha, Lúcia, Agnéte, Cæcília, Anastásia, et
ómnibus Sanctis tuis: intra quorum nos consórtium, non
æstimátor mériti, sed véniæ, quǽsumus, largítor ad-
mítte. Per Christum Dóminum nostrum.

Per quem hæc ómnia, Dómine, semper bona creas, sanc-
tíficas ✠, vivíficas ✠, benedícis ✠, et præstas nobis.

Per ipsum ✠, et cum ipso ✠, et in ipso ✠ est tibi Deo Patri
✠ omnipoténti in unitáte Spíritus ✠ Sancti omnis honor,
et glória, **per ómnia sǽcula sæculórum.**
M: Amen.

countenance, and accept them, as once thou wast pleased to accept the gifts of thy servant Abel, the just, the sacrifice of Abraham our father in faith, and the offering of thy high priest Melchizedek, a holy sacrifice, a spotless victim.

In humble prayer we ask thee, almighty God: command that these gifts be borne by the hands of thy holy Angel to thine altar on high in the sight of thy divine majesty, that all of us who through this participation at the altar receive the most holy Body ✠ and Blood ✠ of thy Son may be filled with every grace and heavenly blessing. Through the same Christ our Lord. Amen.

Remember also, Lord, thy servants and handmaids N. and N. who have gone before us with the sign of faith and rest in the sleep of peace.

Grant them, O Lord, we pray, and all who sleep in Christ, a place of refreshment, light and peace. Through the same Christ our Lord. Amen.

To us, also, thy sinful servants who hope in thy abundant mercies, graciously grant some share and fellowship with thy holy Apostles and Martyrs: with John, Stephen, Matthias, Barnabas, Ignatius, Alexander, Marcellinus, Peter, Felicity, Perpetua, Agatha, Lucy, Agnes, Cecilia, Anastasia and all thy Saints: admit us, we beseech thee, into their company, not weighing our merits, but granting us thy pardon, through Christ our Lord.

Through whom thou dost continue to create all these good things, O Lord; thou dost make them ✠ holy, fill them ✠ with life, bless ✠ them, and bestow them upon us.

Through ✠ him, and with ✠ him, and in ✠ him, to thee, O God, almighty ✠ Father, in the unity of the Holy ✠ Ghost, is all honour and glory, **for ever and ever.**
M: Amen.

Communio

S: Orémus.

Præcéptis salutáribus móniti, et divína institutióne formáti, audémus dícere:

Pater noster, qui es in cælis: Sanctificétur nomen tuum: Advéniat regnum tuum: Fiat volúntas tua, sicut in cælo, et in terra. Panem nostrum cotidiánum da nobis hódie: Et dimítte nobis débita nostra, sicut et nos dimíttimus debitóribus nostris. Et ne nos indúcas in tentatiónem.

M: Sed líbera nos a malo.

S: Amen.

Líbera nos, quǽsumus, Dómine, ab ómnibus malis, prætéritis, præséntibus et futúris: et intercedénte beáta et gloriósa semper Vírgine Dei Genetríce María, cum beátis Apóstolis tuis Petro et Paulo, atque Andréa, et ómnibus Sanctis, da propítius pacem in diébus nostris: ut, ope misericórdiæ tuæ adiúti, et a peccáto simus semper líberi, et ab omni perturbatióne secúri. Per eúndem Dóminum nostrum Iesum Christum Fílium tuum, qui tecum vivit et regnat in unitáte Spíritus Sancti Deus, per ómnia sǽcula sæculórum.

M: Amen.

S: Pax ✠ Dómini sit ✠ semper ✠ vobíscum.

M: Et cum spíritu tuo.

Hæc commíxtio, et consecrátio Córporis et Sánguinis Dómini nostri Iesu Christi, fiat accipiéntibus nobis in vitam ætérnam. Amen.

Agnus Dei, qui tollis peccáta mundi: miserére nobis.

Agnus Dei, qui tollis peccáta mundi: miserére nobis.

Agnus Dei, qui tollis peccáta mundi: dona nobis pacem.

Domine Iesu Christe, qui dixísti Apóstolis tuis: Pacem relínquo vobis, pacem meam do vobis: ne respícias peccáta mea, sed fidem Ecclésiæ tuæ; eámque secúndum

Communion Rites

P: Let us pray.

At the Saviour's command and formed by divine teaching, we dare to say:

Our Father who art in heaven, hallowed be thy name; thy kingdom come, thy will be done on earth as it is in heaven. Give us this day our daily bread, and forgive us our trespasses, as we forgive those who trespass against us; and lead us not into temptation.

R: But deliver us from evil.

P: Amen.

Deliver us, Lord, we pray, from every evil, past, present and to come, and by the intercession of the blessed and glorious ever-Virgin Mary, Mother of God, with thy blessed Apostles Peter and Paul, and Andrew, and all the Saints, graciously grant peace in our days, that, by the help of thy mercy, we may be always free from sin and safe from all distress. Through the same Jesus Christ thy Son our Lord, who lives and reigns with thee in the unity of the Holy Ghost, one God, for ever and ever.

M: Amen

P: The peace ✠ of the Lord be ✠ with you ✠ always.

M: And with thy spirit.

May this mingling and consecration of the Body and Blood of our Lord Jesus Christ bring eternal life to us who receive it. Amen.

Lamb of God, who takest away the sins of the world, have mercy on us.

Lamb of God, who takest away the sins of the world, have mercy on us.

Lamb of God, who takest away the sins of the world, grant us peace.

Lord Jesus Christ, who said to thy Apostles, Peace I leave you, my peace I give you; look not on my sins but on the faith of thy Church; and graciously grant her peace and

voluntátem tuam pacificáre et coadunáre dignéris: Qui vivis et regnas Deus per ómnia sǽcula sæculérum. Amen.

At High Mass
S: Pax tecum.
D: Et cum spíritu tuo.

Dómine Iesu Christe, Fili Dei vivi, qui ex voluntáte Patris, cooperánte Spíritu sancto, per mortem tuam mundum vivificásti: líbera me per hoc sacrosánctum Corpus et Sánguinem tuum ab ómnibus iniquitátibus meis, et univérsis malis: et fac me tuis semper inhærére mandátis, et a te numquam separári permíttas: Qui cum eódem Deo Patre et Spíritu Sancto vivis et regnas Deus in sǽcula sæculórum. Amen.

Percéptio Corpóris tui, Dómine Iesu Christe, quod ego indígnus súmere prǽsumo, non mihi provéniat in iudícium et condemnatiónem: sed pro tua pietáte prosit mihi ad tutaméntum mentis et córporis, et ad medélam percipiéndam: Qui vivis et regnas cum Deo Patre in unitáte Spíritus Sancti Deus, per ómnia sǽcula sæculórum. Amen.
Panem cæléstem accípiam, et nomen Dómini invocábo.

Dómine, non sum dignus, ut intres sub tectum meum: sed tantum dic verbo et sanábitur ánima mea. (*ter*)

Corpus Dómini nostri Iesu Christi custódiat ánimam meam in vitam ætérnam. Amen.
Quid retríbuam Dómino pro ómnibus quæ retríbuit mihi? Cálicem salutáris accípiam, et nomen Dómini invocábo. Laudans invocábo Dóminum, et ab inimícis meis salvus ero.

Sanguis Dómini nostri Iesu Christi custódiat ánimam meam in vitam ætérnam. Amen.

Ecce Agnus Dei: ecce qui tollit peccáta mundi.

unity in accordance with thy will. Who livest and reignest God, for ever and ever. Amen.

> *At High Mass*
> *P:* Peace be with thee.
> *D:* And with thy spirit.

Lord Jesus Christ, Son of the living God, who by the will of the Father and the work of the Holy Ghost, through thy death gavest life to the world, free me by this thy most holy Body and Blood from all my sins and from every evil; keep me always faithful to thy commandments, and never let me be parted from thee; who with the same God the Father and the Holy Ghost livest and reignest God, for ever and ever. Amen.

May the receiving of thy Body and Blood, Lord Jesus Christ, which I though unworthy presume to take, not bring me to judgment and condemnation, but through thy loving mercy may it be for me protection in mind and body; who livest and reignest with God the Father in the unity of the Holy Ghost, God, for ever and ever. Amen.
I will take the bread of heaven, and call upon the name of the Lord.
Lord, I am not worthy that thou shouldst enter under my roof; but only say the word and my soul shall be healed. *(three times)*
May the body of our Lord Jesus Christ keep my soul safe unto eternal life. Amen.

What shall I render to the Lord for all the things he hath rendered to me? I will take the chalice of salvation, and will call upon the name of the Lord. With praise I will call upon the Lord, and I shall be saved from my enemies.

May the Blood of our Lord Jesus Christ keep my soul safe unto eternal life. Amen.

Behold the Lamb of God, behold him who takes away the sins of the world.

Dómine, non sum dignus ut intres sub tectum meum; sed tantum dic verbo et sanábitur ánima mea. *(ter)*

(Sacerdos porrigens Sacramentum, simul dixit:)
Corpus Dómini nostri Iesu Christi custódiat ánimam tuam in vitam ætérnam. Amen.

Postcommunio

Quod ore súmpsimus, Dómine, pura mente capiámus: et de múnere temporáli fiat nobis remédium sempitérnum.

Corpus tuum, Dómine, quod sumpsi, et Sanguis, quem potávi, adhǽreat viscéribus meis: et præsta, ut in me non remáneat scélerum mácula, quem pura et sancta refecérunt sacraménta: Qui vivis et regnas in sǽcula sæculórum. Amen.

Communion antiphon: see Propers

S: Dóminus vobíscum.
M: Et cum spíritu tuo.
S: Oremus.

Postcommunion prayer: see Propers

M: Amen.
S: Dóminus vobíscum.
M: Et cum spíritu tuo.
S/D: Ite, missa est. [*vel:* Benedicamus Domino.]
M: Deo grátias.
Pláceat tibi, sancta Trínitas, obséquium servitútis meæ: et præsta: ut sacrifícium, quod óculis tuæ maiestátis indígnus óbtuli, tibi sit acceptábile, mihíque et ómnibus, pro quibus illud óbtuli, sit, te miseránte, propitiábile. Per Christum Dóminum nostrum. Amen.
> *At Pontifical Mass*
> *Episcopus:* Sit nomen Dómini benedíctum.

Lord, I am not worthy that thou shouldst enter under my roof, but only say the word and my soul shall be healed.
(three times)
(When giving Holy Communion, the Priest says:)
May the Body of our Lord Jesus Christ keep thy soul safe unto eternal life. Amen.

Prayers after Communion

What has passed our lips as food, O Lord, may we possess in purity of heart, that what has been given to us in time may be our healing for eternity.

May thy Body, Lord, which I have received, and thy Blood which I have drunk, cleave to my inmost parts, and grant that no stain of sin may remain in me, whom these pure and holy sacraments have refreshed. Who livest and reignest for ever and ever. Amen.

P: The Lord be with you.
M: And with thy spirit.
P: Let us pray.

M: Amen.
P: The Lord be with you.
M: And with thy spirit.
P. Go, you are dismissed. [*Or:* Let us bless the Lord.]
M: Thanks be to God.
May the tribute of my homage be pleasing to thee, most holy Trinity; and grant that the sacrifice which I, unworthy as I am, have offered in the sight of thy majesty may be acceptable to thee; and through thy mercy may it bring forgiveness to me and all for whom I have offered it. Through Christ our Lord. Amen.
> *At Pontifical Mass*
> *Bishop:* Blessed be the name of the Lord.

Omnes: Ex hoc nunc et usque in sǽculum.
E: Adiutórium nostrum in nómine Dómini.
O: Qui fecit cælum et terram.

Benedicat vos omnípotens Deus, Pater, et Filíus ✠, et Spíritus Sanctus.
M: Amen.

Ultimum Evangelium

S: Dóminus vobíscum.
M: Et cum spíritu tuo.
S: ✠ Inítium sancti Evangélii secúndum Ioánnem.

M: Glória tibi, Dómine.

S: In princípio erat Verbum, et Verbum erat apud Deum, et Deus erat Verbum. Hoc erat in princípio apud Deum. Omnia per ipsum facta sunt: et sine ipso factum est nihil, quod factum est: in ipso vita erat, et vita erat lux hóminum: et lux in ténebris lucet, et ténebræ eam non comprehendérunt.

Fuit homo missus a Deo, cui nomen erat Ioánnes. Hic venit in testimónium, ut testimónium perhibéret de lúmine, ut omnes créderent per illum. Non erat ille lux, sed ut testimónium perhibéret de lúmine. Erat lux vera, quæ illúminat omnem hóminem veniéntem in hunc mundum. In mundo erat, et mundus per ipsum factus est, et mundus eum non cognóvit. In própria venit, et sui eum non recepérunt. Quotquot autem recepérunt eum, dedit eis potestátem fílios Dei fieri, his, qui credunt in nómine eius: qui non ex sanguínibus, neque ex voluntáte carnis, neque ex voluntáte viri, sed ex Deo nati sunt. **ET VERBUM CARO FACTUM EST**, et habitávit in nobis: et vídimus glóriam eius, glóriam quasi Unigéniti a Patre, plenum grátiæ et veritátis.

M: Deo grátias.

All: From henceforth, now and forever.
B.: Our help is in the name of the Lord.
All: Who made heaven and earth.
May almighty God bless you, the Father, the Son ✠, and the Holy Ghost.
M: Amen.

The Last Gospel

P: The Lord be with you.
M: And with thy spirit.
P: ✠ The beginning of the holy Gospel according to John.
M: Glory to thee, O Lord.

P: In the beginning was the Word, and the Word was with God, and the Word was God. The same was in the beginning with God. All things were made by him, and without him was made nothing that was made. In him was life, and the life was the light of men: and the light shineth in darkness, and the darkness did not comprehend it.

There was a man sent from God, whose name was John. This man came for a witness, to bear witness of the light, that all men through him might believe. He was not the light, but was to bear witness of the light. That was the true light, which enlighteneth every man, that cometh into this world. He was in the world, and the world was made by him, and the world knew him not. He came unto his own, and his own received him not. But as many as received him, to them gave he power to be made the sons of God: to them that believe in his name: who were born, not of blood, nor of the will of the flesh, nor of the will of man, but of God. **AND THE WORD WAS MADE FLESH**, and dwelt among us: and we saw his glory, the glory as of the Only Begotten of the Father, full of grace and truth.
M: Thanks be to God.

Oratio pro Reginem

*To follow the Principal Mass on Sunday
in England & Wales*

Cantor: Dómine, salvam fac
Omnes: Reginam nostram Elísabeth, et exáudi nos in die,
qua invocavérimus te.
S: Oremus.
Quǽsumus, omnípotens Deus, ut famula tua Elísabeth,
Regína nostra, quæ tua miseratióne suscépit regni guber-
nácula, virtútum étiam ómnium percípiat increménta;
quibus decénter ornáta et vitiórum monstra devitáre, (*in
time of war:* hostes superáre), et ad te qui via, véritas, et
vita es, cum Principe consorte et prole régia gratiósa
valeat perveníre. Per Christum Dóminum nostrum.

R: Amen.

Omine, salvam fac * regínam nostram E-lí-sa-beth :
For the King: salvam fac * re- gem nostrum

et exáudi nos in di-e, qua invocavé- rimus te.

A Spiritual Communion

My Jesus, I believe that thou art present in the Most Holy
Sacrament. I love thee above all things, and I desire to
receive thee in my soul. Since I cannot at this moment
receive thee sacramentally, come at least spiritually into
my heart. I embrace thee as if thou wert already there, and
unite myself wholly to thee. Never permit me to be
separated from thee. Amen.

Prayer for the Queen

*To follow the Principal Mass on Sunday
in England & Wales*

Cantor: O Lord, save
All: Elizabeth our Queen, and mercifully hear us when we call upon thee.
P: Let us pray.
We beseech thee, almighty God, that thy servant Elizabeth our Queen, who through thy mercy has undertaken the government of this realm, may also receive an increase of all virtues. Fittingly adorned with these, may she be able to shun all evildoing, [*in time of war*: to vanquish her enemies,] and, together with the Prince her consort and the royal family, being in thy grace, to come unto thee who art the way, the truth, and the life. Through Christ our Lord.
R: Amen.

The Memorare

Remember, O most sweet and loving Virgin Mary, that it is a thing unheard of that anyone who fled to thy protection, implored thy help or sought thy intercession was left forsaken. Filled therefore with confidence in thy goodness I fly to thee O Virgin of Virgins, my mother. To thee I come, before thee I stand, a sorrowful sinner. Despise not my words, o mother of the Word, but graciously hear and grant my prayer. Amen.

Orationes Post Missam

S: Ave María, grátia plena, Dóminus tecum; benedícta tu in muliéribus, et benedíctus fructus ventris tui, Iesus.

R: Sancta María, Mater Dei, ora pro nobis peccatóribus, nunc et in hora mortis nostræ. Amen. *(ter)*

Salve Regína, Mater misericórdiæ; vita, dulcédo et spes nostra, salve. Ad te clamámus, éxsules filii Evæ. Ad te suspirámus, geméntes et flentes in hac lacrimarum valle. Eia ergo, advocáta nostra, illos tuos misericórdes óculos ad nos convérte. Et Iesum, benedíctum fructum ventris tui, nobis, post hoc exsílium, osténde. O clemens, o pia, o dulcis Virgo María .
S: Ora pro nobis, sancta Dei Génetrix.
R: Ut digni efficiámur promissiónibus Christi.

S: Orémus
Deus, refúgium nostrum et virtus, pópulum ad te clamántem propítius réspice; et intercedénte gloriósa et immaculáta Virgine Dei Genetríce María, cum beáto Ioseph, eius Sponso, ac beátis Apóstolis tuis Petro et Paulo, et ómnibus Sanctis, quas pro conversióne peccatórum, pro libertáte et exaltatióne sanctæ Matris Ecclésiæ, preces effúndimus, miséricors et benígnus exáudi. Per eúndem Christum Dóminum nostrum.
R: Amen.

S: Sancte Míchaéle Archángele, defénde nos in proélio, contra nequítiam et insídias diáboli esto præsídium. Imperet illi Deus, súpplices deprecámur: tuque, princeps milítiæ cæléstis, Sátanam aliósque spíritus malígnos, qui ad perditiónem animárum pervagántur in mundo, divína virtúte in inférnum detrúde.
R: Amen.

S: Cor Iesu sacratíssimum,
R: Miserére nobis. *(ter)*

Prayers After Low Mass

P: Hail, Mary, full of grace, the Lord is with thee; blessed art thou amongst women, and blessed is the fruit of thy womb, Jesus.

R: Holy Mary, Mother of God, pray for us sinners, now and at the hour of our death. Amen. *(three times)*

Hail, holy Queen, Mother of mercy; hail, our life, our sweetness and our hope. To thee do we cry, poor banished children of Eve. To thee do we send up our sighs, mourning and weeping in this vale of tears. Turn then, most gracious advocate, thine eyes of mercy towards us. And after this our exile, show unto us the blessed fruit of thy womb, Jesus. O clement, O loving, O sweet Virgin Mary.

P: Pray for us, O holy Mother of God.

R: That we may be made worthy of the promises of Christ.

P: Let us pray.

O God, our refuge and our strength, look down in mercy on thy people who cry to thee; and by the intercession of the glorious and immaculate Virgin Mary, Mother of God, of St Joseph her spouse, of thy blessed Apostles Peter and Paul, and of all the saints, in mercy and goodness hear our prayers for the conversion of sinners, and for the liberty and exaltation of our holy Mother the Church. Through the same Christ our Lord.

R: Amen.

P: Holy Michael Archangel, defend us in the day of battle; be our safeguard against the wickedness and snares of the devil. May God rebuke him, we humbly pray, and do thou, prince of the heavenly host, by the power of God thrust down to hell Satan and all wicked spirits, who wander through the world for the ruin of souls.

R: Amen.

P: Most Sacred Heart of Jesus,

R: Have mercy on us. *(three times)*

PREFACES

The Common Preface is on pp20-1

Preface of Trinity Sunday
used on most Sundays

Vere dignum et iustum est, æquum et salutáre, nos tibi semper, et ubíque grátias ágere: Dómine, sancte Pater, omnípotens ætérne Deus: Qui cum uni-génito Fílio tuo et Spíritu Sancto, unus es Deus, unus es Dóminus: non in uníus singular-itáte persónæ, sed in uníus Trinitáte substántiæ. Quod enim de tua glória, revelánte te, crédimus, hoc de Fílio tuo, hoc de Spíritu Sancto, sine differéntia discretiónis sentímus. Ut in confessióne veræ sempiternǽque Deitátis, et in persónis pro-príetas, et in esséntia únitas, et in maiestáte adorétur æquálitas. Quam laudant Angeli atque Archángeli, Ché-rubim quoque ac Séraphim: qui non ces-sant clamáre cotídie, una voce dicéntes:

It is truly right and just, our duty and our salva-tion, always and every-where to give thee thanks, Lord, holy Father, al-mighty and eternal God. For with thy only begot-ten Son and the Holy Ghost thou art one God, one Lord: not in the unity of a single person, but in a Trinity of one sub-stance. For what thou hast revealed to us of thy glo-ry, we believe equally of thy Son and of the Holy Ghost without difference or distinction, so that, in the confessing of the true and eternal Godhead, thou mayest be adored in what is proper to each Person, their unity in substance, and their equality in majesty. For this is praised by Angels and Archangels, Cheru-bim too, and Seraphim, who never cease to cry out each day, as with one voice they acclaim:

Preface of the Blessed Virgin Mary

Vere dignum et iustum est, æquum et salutáre, nos tibi semper et ubíque grátias ágere: Dómine, sancte Pater, omnípotens ætérne Deus: Et te in [Veneratióne, *vel* Festivitáte *etc.*] beátæ Maríæ semper Vírginis collaudáre, benedícere et prædicáre. Quæ et Unigénitum tuum Sancti Spíritus obumbratióne concépit: et, virginitátis glória permanénte, lumen ætérnum mundo effúdit, Iesum Christum, Dóminum nostrum. Per quem maiestátem tuam laudant Angeli, adórant Dominatiónes, tremunt Potestátes. Cæli cælorúmque Virtútes ac beáta Séraphim sócia exsultatióne concélebrant. Cum quibus et nostras voces ut admítti iúbeas, deprecámur, súpplici confessióne dicéntes:

It is truly right and just, our duty and our salvation, always and everywhere to give thee thanks, Lord, holy Father, almighty and eternal God, and to praise, bless, and glorify thy name in [veneration *or* the festival *etc.*] of the Blessed ever-virgin Mary. For by the overshadowing of the Holy Ghost she conceived thy Only Begotten Son, and, without losing the glory of virginity, brought forth into the world the eternal Light, Jesus Christ our Lord. Through him the Angels praise thy majesty, Dominions adore and Powers tremble before thee. Heaven and the Virtues of heaven and the blessed Seraphim worship together with exultation. May our voices, we pray, join with theirs in humble praise as we acclaim:

Preface of the Apostles

Vere dignum et iustum est, æquum et salutare: Te, Domine, supplicitur exorare, ut gregem tuum, Pastor æterne, non deseras: sed per beatos Apostolos tuos continua protectione custodias. Ut iisdem rectoribus gubernetur, quos operis tui vicarios eidem contulisti præesse pastores. Et ideo cum Angelis et Archangelis, cum Thronis et Dominationibus, cumque omni militia cælestis exercitus, hymnum gloriæ tuæ canimus, sine fine dicentes:

It is truly right and just, our duty and our salvation, to entreat thee humbly, Lord, that thou, eternal Shepherd, desert not thy flock, but through the blessed Apostles watch over it and protect it always, so that it may be governed by those thou hast appointed shepherds to lead it in thy name. And so, with Angels and Archangels, with Thrones and Dominions, and with all the hosts and Powers of heaven, as we sing the hymn of thy glory without end we acclaim:

41

Ritus Aspersionis

at the beginning of the Principal Mass on Sundays

Sacerdos: Aspérges me
Omnes: Dómine, hyssópo, et mundábor: lavábis me, et super nivem dealbábor.
Cantores: Miserére mei, Deus,
Omnes: secúndum magnam misericórdiam tuam.
Cantores: Glória Patri, et Fílio, et Spirítui Sancto,

Omnes: Sicut erat in princípio, et nunc, et semper, et in sæcula sæculórum. Amen. Aspérges me...

S: Osténde nobis, Dómine, misericórdiam tuam.
R: Et salutáre tuum da nobis.
S: Dómine, exáudi oratiónem meam.
R: Et clamor meus ad te véniat.
S: Dóminus vobíscum.
R: Et cum spíritu tuo.

S: Oremus.
Exáudi nos, Dómine, sancte Pater, omnípotens ætérne Deus: et míttere dignéris sanctum Ángelum tuum de cælis, qui custódiat, fóveat, prótegat, vísitet, atque deféndat omnes habitántes in hoc habitáculo. Per Christum Dóminum nostrum.
R: Amen.

During Eastertide the Antiphon and Verse are as follows:

Sacerdos: Vidi aquam
Omnes: egrediéntem de templo, a látere dextro, allelúia: et omnes ad quos pervénit aqua ista salvi facti sunt, et dicent: allelúia, allelúia.
Cantores: Confitémini Dómino, quóniam bonus;
Omnes: quóniam in sæculum misericórdia eius.
Cantores: Glória Patri, et Fílio, et Spirítui Sancto,

Omnes: Sicut erat in princípio, et nunc, et semper, et in sæcula sæculórum. Amen. Vidi aquam...
S: Ostende nobis ... [*as above*]

Asperges *or* Vidi Aquam

at the beginning of the Principal Mass on Sundays

Priest: Thou shalt sprinkle me
All: With hyssop, O Lord, and I shall be cleansed; thou shalt wash me, and I shall be made whiter than snow.
Cantors: Have mercy on me, O God,
All: according to thy great mercy.
Cantors: Glory be to the Father and to the Son and to the Holy Ghost.
All: As it was in the beginning, is now, and ever shall be, world without end. Amen. Thou shalt sprinkle me...

P: Show us, O Lord, thy mercy.
R: And grant us thy salvation.
P: Lord, hear my prayer.
R: And let my cry come unto thee.
P: The Lord be with you.
R: And with thy spirit.

P: Let us pray.
Graciously hear us, Lord, holy Father, almighty and eternal God; and be pleased to send thy holy Angel from heaven to watch over, to cherish, to protect, to abide with, and to defend all who dwell in this house. Through Christ our Lord.

R: Amen.

During Eastertide the Antiphon and Verse are as follows:

Priest: I saw water
All: flowing from the right side of the Temple, alleluia: and all to whom that water came were saved, and they shall say: alleluia, alleluia.
Cantors: Give praise to the Lord, for he is good,
All: for his mercy endures forever.
Cantors: Glory be to the Father and to the Son and to the Holy Ghost.
All: As it was in the beginning, is now, and ever shall be, world without end. Amen. I saw water …
P: Show us, … [*as above*]

CHANTS FOR THE MASS

Asperges

*Sung at the beginning of Mass, on the principal Sung
Mass on a Sunday, except during Eastertide.*

Ant. 7. / XIII. s.

A-Spérges me, * Dómi-ne, hyssó-po, et mundábor: lavá- bis me, et su-per nivem de- albá- bor.

Ps.50. Mi- se-rére me-i, De- us, * se-cúndum magnam mise-
ricórdi- am tu- am. Gló- ri- a Patri, et Fí-li- o, et Spi-rí-
tu- i Sancto: * Sic- ut e-rat in princí-pi- o, et nunc, et
semper, et in sǽcula sæcu-lórum. A-men. *Repeat Ant.*

℣. Osténde nobis, Dómine, misericórdiam tuam.
℟. Et salutáre tuam da nobis.
℣. Dómine exáudi oratiónem meam.
℟. Et clamor meus ad te véniat.
℣. Dóminus vobíscum.
℟. Et cum spíritu tuo.
℣. Orémus. …. Per Dn nostrum.
℟. Amen.

Vidi Aquam

Sung in place of the Asperges, in Eastertide

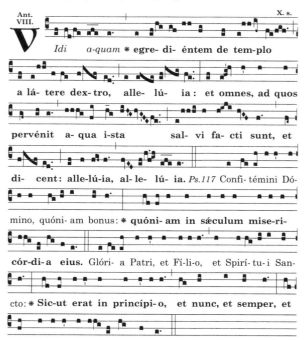

Vidi aquam * egrediéntem de templo a látere dextro, allelúia : et omnes, ad quos pervénit aqua ista salvi facti sunt, et dicent: allelúia, allelúia. *Ps.117* Confitémini Dómino, quóniam bonus: * quóniam in sǽculum misericórdia eius. Glória Patri, et Fílio, et Spirítui Sancto: * Sicut erat in princípio, et nunc, et semper, et in sǽcula sæculórum. Amen. *Repeat Ant.* Vidi aquam.

℣. Osténde nobis, Dómine, misericórdiam tuam.
℟. Et salutáre tuam da nobis.
℣. Dómine exáudi oratiónem meam.
℟. Et clamor meus ad te véniat.
℣. Dóminus vobíscum.
℟. Et cum spíritu tuo.
℣.Orémus. …. Per Dn nostrum.
℟. Amen.

IV. IN FESTIS DUPLICIBUS. I.
(Cunctipotens Genitor Deus)

Ký-ri- e * e- lé- i-son. *iii.* Chri-

ste e- lé- i-son. *iii.* Ký-ri- e e- lé- i-

son. *ii* Ký-ri- e * ** e- lé- i-son.

Ló- ri- a in excélsis De- o. Et in terra pax homí-ni-

bus bonæ vo-luntá-tis. **Laudámus te.** Bene- dí-ci-mus te.

Adorá- mus te. Glo-ri-ficá- mus te. **Gráti- as ágimus**

tibi propter magnam gló-ri- am tu-am. Dómi-ne De-us,

Rex cæ-léstis, De- us Pa- ter omní- potens. **Dómine Fi-li**

uni-géni- te Ie- su Chri- ste. Dómi-ne De-us, Agnus

De- i, Fí- li-us Pa- tris. **Qui tollis peccáta mundi, mise-**

ré-re nobis. Qui tollis peccáta mundi, súscipe depreca-ti- ó-

nem nostram. **Qui sedes ad déxteram Patris, mi-se-rére**

46

nobis. Quóni- am tu solus sanctus. **Tu solus Dóminus.** Tu

solus Altíssimus Ie- su Chri- ste. **Cum Sancto Spí-**

ri- tu, in glóri- a De-i Pa- tris. A-   men.

XI. s.

VIII.

S An- ctus, * Sanctus, San- ctus, Dóminus De-us Sá-

ba-oth Pleni sunt cæli et terra gló- ri- a tu- a. Ho- sánna

in ex- cél- sis. Bene-díctus qui ve-nit in nómine Dó

mi-ni. Ho-   sánna in ex- cél-   sis.

(XII) XIII. s.

VI.

A -gnus De- i, * qui tollis peccáta mundi: mise-ré- re

no- bis. Agnus De- i, * qui tollis peccáta mundi: mise-ré- re

no- bis. Agnus De- i, * qui tollis peccáta mundi: dona no-

bis pa- cem.

I.

I - te,   missa est.
De- o   grá- ti- as.

IX. IN FESTIS B. MARIÆ VIRGINIS. I.
(Cum iubilo)

Ký- ri- e * e-lé- i-son. Ký-ri- e e-lé- i-son

Ký- ri- e e-lé- i-son. Christe e- lé- i-son. Chri-

ste e-lé- i-son. Christe e-lé- i-son. Ký-ri- e

e-lé- i-son. Ký- ri- e e-lé- i-son. Ký-ri- e *

** e-lé- i-son.

Ló- ri- a in excélsis De- o. Et in terra pax homí-ni-

bus bonæ voluntá- tis. **Laudámus te.** Bene- dí-cimus te.

Ado- rá-mus te. Glo-ri-ficá-mus te. **Gráti-as ágimus tibi**

propter magnam glóri- am tu- am. Dómine De- us, Rex

cæ- léstis, De-us Pa-ter omnípot- ens. **Dómine Fi-li unigé-**

nite, Ie-su Christe. Dó-mi-ne De-us, Agnus De- i, Fí-li-us

Patris. **Qui tollis peccáta mundi, miseré-re nobis.** Qui tollis peccáta mundi, sús- cipe depreca-ti-ó-nem nostram. **Qui
sedes ad déxteram Patris, miseré-re nobis.** Quóni- am tu
solus Sanctus. **Tu solus Dóminus.** Tu solus Altíssimus Iesu
Chri-ste. **Cum Sancto Spí-ritu, in glóri-a De-i Pa- tris.**
A- men.

(XI) XII. s.

V. S An- ctus, * Sanctus, San- ctus, Dóminus De- us
Sá- ba- oth. Pleni sunt cæ-li et ter- ra glóri- a tu- a.
Hosán-na in excél-sis. Be- nedíctus qui ve- nit in nó- mi-
ne Dó- mi- ni. Ho- sánna in ex-cél- sis.

XV. s.

V. A -gnus De- i, * qui tol- lis peccá-ta mun- di: mi-
se- ré-re no- bis. Agnus De- i, * qui tol- lis peccá-ta mun-

49

di: mi-se- ré- re no- bis. Agnus De- i, * qui tol- lis pec-

cá-ta mun- di: do-na no- bis pa- cem.

I.

I - te, missa est.
De- o grá- ti- as.

XI. IN DOMINICIS INFRA ANNUM
(Orbis factor)

(X) XIV-XVI. s.

I.

KÝ-ri- e * e- lé- i-son. *iii.* Chri- ste

e- lé- i-son. *iii.* Ký-ri- e * e- lé- i-son. *ii.* Ký- ri-

e e- lé- i-son.

II. X. s.

GLÓ-ri- a in excélsis De- o. Et in terra pax homíni

bus bonae voluntá-tis. **Laudámus te.** Benedí- cimus te.

Adorámus te. Glori-fi-cámus te. **Gráti-as ágimus ti-**

bi propter magnam glóri-am tu-am. Dómi-ne De- us, Rex

cæléstis, De-us Pater omní-potens. **Dómine Fi- li unigéni-**

50

te, Ie-su Christe. Dómi-ne De-us, Agnus De-i, Fí-li-us

Patris. **Qui tollis peccáta mundi, mise-rére nobis.** Qui tol-

lis peccá-ta mun-di, súscipe depreca-ti-ónem nostram. **Qui**

sedes ad déxteram Patris, mise-rére nobis. Quóni-am

tu solus Sanctus. **Tu solus Dóminus.** Tu so-lus Altíssimus

Ie-su Christe. **Cum Sancto Spíri-tu, in glóri-a De-i**

Pa- tris. A-men.

XI. s.

II.

S anctus, ✱ San-ctus, Sanctus, Dóminus De-us Sá-ba-

oth. Ple-ni sunt cae-li et ter-ra gló-ri-a tu-a. Ho-sán-

na in ex-célsis. Benedíctus qui ve-nit in nó-mine Dó-

mi-ni. Hosánna in ex-célsis.

XIV. s.

I.

A - gnus De-i, ✱ qui tollis peccá-ta mundi: miseré-re

nobis. Agnus De-i, �)(qui tol- lis peccá-ta mun-di : miseré- re

nobis. Agnus Dei, ✻ qui tollis pec-cá- ta mundi : do-na no-

bis pacem.

I.

- te, mis- sa est.
De- o grá- ti- as.

CREDO I

XI. s.

IV.

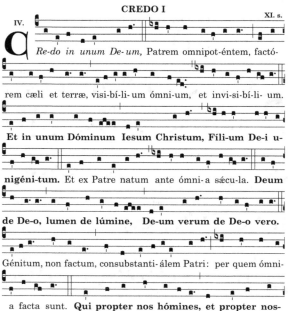

Re-do in unum De-um, Patrem omnipot-éntem, factó-

rem cæli et terræ, visi-bí-li- um ómni-um, et invi-si-bí-li- um.

Et in unum Dóminum Iesum Christum, Fíli-um De-i u-

nigéni-tum. Et ex Patre natum ante ómni-a sǽcu-la. **Deum**

de De-o, lumen de lúmine, De-um verum de De-o vero.

Génitum, non factum, consubstanti-álem Patri: per quem ómni-

a facta sunt. **Qui propter nos hómines, et propter nos-**

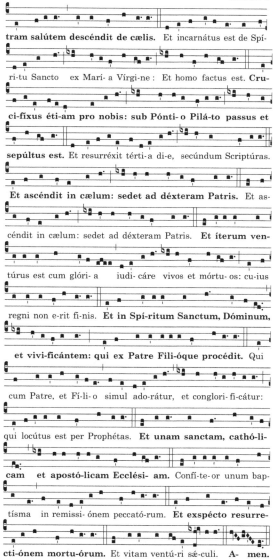

tram salútem descéndit de cælis. Et incarnátus est de Spí-

ri-tu Sancto   ex Marí- a Vírgi-ne : Et homo factus est. **Cru-**

ci-fíxus éti-am pro nobis: sub Pónti- o Pilá-to passus et

sepúltus est. Et resurréxit térti- a di-e, secúndum Scriptúras.

Et ascéndit in cælum: sedet ad déxteram Patris. Et as-

céndit in cælum: sedet ad déxteram Patris. **Et íterum ven-**

túrus est cum glóri- a   iudi- cáre vivos et mórtu- os: cu-ius

regni non e-rit fi-nis. **Et in Spí-ritum Sanctum, Dóminum,**

et vivi-ficántem: qui ex Patre Fili-óque procédit. Qui

cum Patre, et Fí-li- o simul ado-rátur, et conglori- fi-cátur:

qui locútus est per Prophétas. **Et unam sanctam, cathó-li-**

cam   et apostó-licam Ecclési- am. Confí-te- or unum bap-

tísma in remissi- ónem peccató-rum. **Et exspécto resurre-**

cti-ónem mortu-órum. Et vitam ventú-ri sæ-culi. A- men.

Marian Anthems

Alma ✶ Redemptóris, Mater, quae pérvi-a cæ-li porta ma-nes, Et stella maris, succúrre cadénti súrgere qui curat pópulo: Tu quæ genu-ísti, natúra mi-ránte, tu-um sanctum Geni-tórem: Virgo pri-us ac postéri-us, Gabri-é-lis ab ore sumens illud Ave peccató-rum mi-se-ré-re.

During Advent:

℣. Ángelus Dómini nuntiávit Maríæ.

℟. Et concépit de Spíritu Sancto.

During Christmastide:

℣. Post pártum Virgo invioláta permansísti.

℟. Dei Génetrix, intercéde pro nobis.

A-ve, Regína cæ-lórum, ✶ Ave, Dómina Ange-lórum: Salve, radix, salve, porta Ex qua mundo lux est orta: Gaude, Virgo glori-ósa, Su-per omnes spe-ci-ósa: Vale, o valde decó-ra, Et pro nobis Christum exó-ra.

℣. Dignáre me laudáre te, Virgo sacráta.

℟. Da míhi virtútem contra hóstes túos.

VI.
Regína cæ-li * læ-táre, alle-lú-ia : Qui-a quem meru-ísti portáre, alle-lú-ia : Resurréxit, sic-ut dixit, alle-lú-ia :
Ora pro no-bis De-um alle-lú- ia :

℣. Gaude et lætáre Virgo María, allelúia.
℟. Quia surréxit Dóminus vere, allelúia.

V.
Alve, Regína, * mater mi-se-ri-córdi-æ : Vi-ta, dulcé-do, et spes nóstra, salve. Ad te clamámus, éxsu-les, fí-li- i Hevæ Ad te suspi-rámus, geméntes et flentes In hac lacrimárum valle E-ia ergo, Advocá-ta nostra, illos tu-os mi-seri-córdes ócu-los ad nos convérte. Et Iesum, bene-díctum fructum ventris tu-i, nobis post hoc exsí-li- um osténde. O clemens : O pi- a : O dulcis Virgo Ma-rí- a.

℣. Ora pro nóbis sáncta Déi Génetrix.
℟. Ut dígni efficiámur promissiónibus Chrísti.

Missa Votiva Pro Peregrinantibus

Rédime me, Dómine, et miserére mei: pes enim meus stetit in via recta: in ecclésiis benedícam Dóminum. V. Iúdica me, Dómine, quóniam ego in innocéntia mea ingréssus sum: et in Dómino sperans, non infirmábor. Glória Patri.

Adésto, Dómine, supplicatiónibus nostris: et viam famulórum tuórum in salútis tuæ prosperitáte dispóne; ut inter omnes viæ et vitæ huius varietátes, tuo semper protegántur auxilio. Per Dominum.

In diébus illis: Egréssus Iacob de Bersabée, pergébat Haran. Cumque venísset ad quendam locum, et vellet in eo requiéscere post solis occúbitum, tulit de lapídibus qui iacébant, et suppónens cápiti suo, dormívit in eódem loco. Vidítque in somnis Dóminum dicéntem sibi: Ego sum Dóminus, Deus Ábraham, patris tui, et Deus Ísaac: terram, in qua dormis, tibi dabo et sémini tuo. Erítque semen tuum quasi pulvis terræ: dilatáberis ad Occidéntem et Oriéntem et Septentriónem et Merídiem: et benedicéntur in te et in sémine tuo cunctæ tribus terræ. Et ero custos tuus, quocúmque perréxeris, et redúcam te in terram hanc; nec dimíttam, nisi complévero univérsa quæ dixi. Surgens ergo Iacob mane, tulit lápidem, quem supposúerat cápiti suo, et eréxit in títulum, fundens óleum désuper. Vovit étiam votum, dicens: Si fúerit Deus mecum et custodíerit me in via, per quam ego ámbulo, et déderit mihi panem ad vescéndum, et vestiméntum ad induéndum, reversúsque fúero próspere ad domum patris mei: erit mihi Dóminus in Deum, et lapis iste, quem eréxi in títulum, vocábitur domus Dei: cunctorúmque, quæ déderis mihi, décimas ófferam tibi.

Si ámbulem in médio umbræ mortis, non timébo mala: quóniam tu mecum es, Dómine. V. Virga tua et báculus tuus, ipsa me consoláta sunt.

Votive Mass for Pilgrims

Ps 25:11-12; 25:1
Redeem me, O Lord, and have pity on me; my foot has
stood in the direct way: in the churches I will bless the
Lord. V. Judge me, O Lord, for I have walked in my innocence; and I have put my trust in the Lord, and shall not
be weakened. Glory be.

Heed our entreaties, Lord, and give thy servants a safe
and prosperous journey. Amid all the hazards of their way
through this life let them ever be sheltered by thy aid:
through our Lord.

Genesis 28: 10-12, 13-15, 18, 20-22
In those days: Jacob being departed from Bersabee, went
on to Haran. And when he was come to a certain place,
and would rest in it after sunset, he took of the stones that
lay there, and putting under his head, slept in the same
place. And he saw in his sleep the Lord saying to him: I
am the Lord God of Abraham thy father, and the God of
Isaac: The land, wherein thou sleepest, I will give to thee
and to thy seed. And thy seed shall be as the dust of the
earth: thou shalt spread abroad to the west, and to the east,
and to the north, and to the south: and in thee and thy
seed, all the tribes of the earth shall be blessed. And I will
be thy keeper whithersoever thou goest, and will bring
thee back into this land: neither will I leave thee, till I
shall have accomplished all that I have said. And Jacob
arising in the morning, took the stone which he had laid
under his head, and set it up for a title, pouring oil upon
the top of it. And he made a vow, saying: If God shall be
with me, and shall keep me in the way, by which I walk,
and shall give me bread to eat, and raiment to put on, And
I shall return prosperously to my father's house: the Lord
shall be my God: And this stone, which I have set up for a
title, shall be called the house of God: and of all things
that thou shalt give to me, I will offer tithes to thee.

Ps 22:4
Though I should walk in the midst of the shadow of
death, I will fear no evils; for thou art with me, O Lord.
V. Thy rod and thy staff: they have comforted me.

ALLELUIA

Alleúia, alleúia. Gressus meos dírige secúndum elóqui-
um tuum: ut non dominétur mei omnis iniustítia. Alleúia.

GOSPEL

In illo témpore: Dixit Iesus discípulis suis: Eúntes,
prædicáte, dicéntes: Quia appropinquávit regnum
cælórum. Infírmos curáte, mórtuos suscitáte, leprósos
mundáte, dǽmones eícite: gratis accepístis, gratis date.
Nolíte possidére aurum neque argéntum neque pecúniam
in zonis vestris: non peram in via, neque duas túnicas,
neque calceaménta, neque virgam: dignus enim est
operárius cibo suo. In quamcúmque autem civitátem aut
castéllum intravéritis, interrogáte, quis in ea dignus sit: et
ibi manéte donec exeátis. Intrántes autem in domum,
salutáte eam, dicéntes: Pax huic dómui. Et si quidem
fúerit domus digna, véniet pax vestra super eam: si autem
non fúerit digna, pax vestra revertétur ad vos. Et
quicúmque non recéperit vos, neque audíerit sermónes
vestros: exeúntes foras de domo vel civitáte, excútite
púlverem de pédibus vestris.

OFFERTORY

Pérfice gressus meos in sémitis tuis, ut non moveántur
vestígia mea: inclína aurem tuam, et exáudi verba mea:
mirífica misericórdias tuas, qui salvos facis sperántes in
te, Dómine.

Common Preface

SECRET

Propitiáre, Dómine, supplicatiónibus nostris, et has oblatiónes, quas tibi offérimus pro fámulis tuis, benígnus
assúme: ut viam illórum et præcedénte grátia tua dírigas
et subsequénte comitári dignéris; ut de actu atque incolu-
mitáte eorum, secúndum misericórdiæ tuæ præsídia,
gaudeámus. Per Dóminum.

COMMUNION

Tu mandásti mandáta tua custodíri nimis: útinam
dirigántur viæ meæ, ad custodiéndas iustificatiónes tuas.

POSTCOMMUNION

Tua, Dómine, sacraménta quæ súmpsimus, fámulos tuos
in te sperántes custódiant: et contra omnes advérsos
tueántur incúrsus. Per Dominum.

Ps 118:133
Alleluia, alleluia. Direct my steps according to thy word:
and let no iniquity have dominion over me. Alleluia.

Matthew 10:7-14
At that time: Jesus said to his disciples: Going, preach,
saying: The kingdom of heaven is at hand. Heal the sick,
raise the dead, cleanse the lepers, cast out devils. Freely
have you received; freely give. Do not possess gold, nor
silver, nor money in your purses, nor scrip for your journey, nor two coats, nor shoes, nor a staff. For the work-
man is worthy of his meat. And into whatsoever city or
town you shall enter, inquire who in it is worthy; and
there abide till you go thence. And, when you come into
the house, salute it, saying: Peace be to this house. And, if
that house be worthy, your peace shall come upon it. But
if it be not worthy, your peace shall return to you. And
whosoever shall not receive you, nor hear your words;
going forth out of that house or city shake off the dust
from your feet.

Ps 16:5, 6-7
Make my steps steadfast in thy paths, that my feet may
not falter. Incline thy ear to me; hear my word. Show thy
wondrous kindness, O Lord, Saviour of those who trust in
thee.

Be appeased, O Lord, by our humble prayers and graciously receive these offerings which we make to thee on
behalf of thy servants: vouchsafe to send thy grace before
them to guide their steps, and to let it follow after them to
accompany them in their path; so that by the protection of
thy mercy, we may rejoice both in their progress and in
their safety. Though our Lord.

Ps. 118, 4-5
Thou hast commanded thy commandments to be kept
most diligently. O that my ways may be directed to keep
thy justifications!

May thy sacraments, O Lord, which we have received,
preserve thy servants who hope in thee; and defend them
from all assaults of the enemy. Through our Lord.

Missa de Sancta Maria in Sabbato

per annum

Salve, sancta Parens, eníxa puérpera Regem: Qui cælum terrámque regit in sǽcula sæculórum. V. Eructávit cor meum verbum bonum : dico ego ópera mea Regi. Glória Patri.

COLLECT

Concéde nos fámulos tuos, quǽsumus, Dómine Deus, perpétua mentis et córporis sanitáte gaudére : et, gloriósa beátæ Maríæ semper Vírginis intercessióne, a præsénti liberári tristítia, et ætérna pérfrui lætítia. Per Dóminum.

LESSON

Ab inítio et ante sǽcula creáta sum, et usque ad futúrum sǽculum non désinam, et in habitatióne sancta coram ipso ministrávi. Et sic in Sion firmáta sum, et in civitáte sanctificáta simíliter requiévi, et in Ierúsalem potéstas mea. Et radicávi in pópulo honorificáto, et in parte Dei mei heréditas illíus, et in plenitúdine sanctórum deténtio mea.

GRADUAL

Benedícta et venerábilis es, Virgo María: quæ sine tactu pudóris, invénta es Mater Salvatóris. V. Virgo Dei Génetrix, quem totus non capit orbis, in tua se clausit víscera factus homo .

ALLELUIA

Allelúia, Allelúia. V. Post partum, Virgo, invioláta permansísti: Dei Génetrix, intercéde pro nobis. Allelúia.

GOSPEL

In illo témpore: Loquénte Iesu ad turbas, extóllens vocem quædam múlier de turba, dixit illi: Beátus venter qui te

Mass of Our Lady on Saturdays

from Trinity Sunday until Advent

Sedulius; Ps. 44: 2
Hail, holy Mother, thou whose child-bearing gave birth to the King who rules heaven and earth for ever and ever. V. My heart hath uttered a good word : I speak my works to the King. Glory be.

Grant, Lord God, that we thy servants may rejoice in unfailing health of mind and body; and through the glorious intercession of Blessed Mary ever-Virgin may we be set free from present sorrow and come to enjoy eternal happiness. Through our Lord.

Eccles. 24. 14-16
From the beginning, and before the world, was I created, and unto the world to come I shall not cease to be, and in the holy dwelling place I have ministered before him. And so I was established in Sion, and in the holy city likewise I rested, and my power was in Jerusalem. And I took root in an honourable people, and in the portion of my God his inheritance, and my abode is in the full assembly of saints.

Blessed and venerable art thou, O Virgin Mary, who with no touch of disgrace wast found the Mother of the Saviour. V. O Virgin Mother of God, he whom the whole world cannot contain hath shut himself within thy womb, becoming man.

Alleluia, alleluia. V. After child-birth, O Virgin, thou didst remain undefiled: O Mother of God, intercede for us. Alleluia

Luke 11:27-28
At that time, as Jesus was speaking to the multitudes, a certain woman from the crowd, lifting up her voice, said

portávit, et úbera quæ suxísti. At ille dixit: Quinímmo beáti qui áudiunt verbum Dei, et custódiunt illud.

Ave, María, grátia plena: Dóminus tecum: benedícta tu in muliéribus, et benedíctus fructus ventris tui.

Tua, Dómine, propitiatióne, et beátæ Maríæ semper Vírginis intercessióne, ad perpétuam atque præséntem hæc oblátio nobis profíciat prosperitátem et pacem. Per Dóminum .

Vere dignum et iustum est, æquum et salutáre, nos tibi semper et ubíque grátias ágere: Dómine, sancte Pater, omnípotens ætérne Deus : Et te in Veneratióne beátæ Maríæ semper Vírginis collaudáre, benedícere et prædicáre. Quæ et Unigénitum tuum Sancti Spíritus obumbratióne concépit : et virginitátis glória permanénte, lumen ætérnum mundo effúdit, Iesum Christum Dóminum nostrum. Per quem maiestátem tuam laudant Ángeli, adórant Dominatiónes, tremunt Potestátes. Cæli cælorúmque Virtútes ac beáta Séraphim, sócia exsultatióne concélebrant. Cum quibus et nostras voces ut admítti iúbeas, deprecámur, súpplici confessióne dicéntes:

Beata víscera Maríæ Vírginis, quæ portavérunt ætérni Patris Fílium.

Sumptis, Dómine, salútis nostræ subsídiis : da, quǽsumus, beátæ Maríæ semper Vírginis patrocíniis nos ubíque prótegi; in cuius venerátione hæc tuæ obtúlimus maiestáti. Per Dóminum.

to him: Blessed is the womb that bore thee and the paps that gave thee suck. But he said: Yea, rather, blessed are they who hear the world of God and keep it.

Luke 1.28, 42
Hail, Mary, full of grace: the Lord is with thee: blessed art thou amongst women, and blessed is the fruit of thy womb.

By thy gracious mercy, Lord, and at the intercession of blessed Mary the ever-Virgin, let this offering bring us prosperity and peace, now and for ever. Through our Lord.

It is truly right and just, our duty and our salvation, always and everywhere to give thee thanks, Lord, holy Father, almighty and eternal God, and to praise, bless, and glorify thy name in veneration of the Blessed ever-virgin Mary. For by the overshadowing of the Holy Ghost she conceived thy only-begotten Son, and, without losing the glory of virginity, brought forth into the world the eternal Light, Jesus Christ our Lord. Through him the Angels praise thy majesty, Dominions adore and Powers tremble before thee. Heaven and the Virtues of heaven and the blessed Seraphim worship together with exultation. May our voices, we pray, join with theirs in humble praise, as we acclaim:

Blessed is the womb of the Virgin Mary, which bore the Son of the Eternal Father.

Grant, we beseech thee, Lord, that we who have received these helps to our salvation may everywhere be sheltered by the patronage of Blessed Mary ever-Virgin, in whose honour we have made these offerings to thy majesty. Through our Lord.

Martyres Universitatis Oxoniensis

INTROIT

Intret in conspectu tuo, Domine; gemitus compeditorum: redde vicinis nostris septuplum in sinu eorum: vindica sanguinem sanctorum tuorum, qui effsus est. V. Deus venerunt gentes in hæreditatem tuam: polluerunt templum sanctum tuum: posuerunt Jerusalem in pomorum custodiam. Gloria Patri.

COLLECT

Deus qui veræ fídei et sedis apostólicæ primátui propugnándo beátos Mártyres tuos Edmúndum ejúsque sócios invícta fortitúdine roborásti eórum précibus exorátus, nostræ, quæsumus, infirmitáti succúrre, ut fortes in fide adversário resístere usque in finem valeámus. Per Dóminum nostrum.

LECTION

In diébus illis : Respóndit unus de senióribus, et dixit mihi : Hi, qui amícti sunt stolis albis, qui sunt? et unde venérunt? Et dixi illi : Dómine mi, tu scis. Et dixit mihi : Hi sunt, qui venérunt de tribulatióne magna, et lavérunt stolas suas, et dealbavérunt eas in sánguine Agni. Ideo sunt ante thronum Dei, et sérviunt ei die ac nocte in templo eius : et qui sedet in throno, habitábit super illos : non esúrient neque sítient ámplius, nec cadet super illos sol neque ullus æstus : quóniam Agnus, qui in médio throni est, reget illos et dedúcet eos ad vitæ fontes aquárum : et abstérget Deus omnem lácrimam ab óculis eórum.

GRADUAL

Gloriosus Deus in Sanctis suis, mirabilis in maiestate. V. Dextera tua, Domine, glorificata est in virtute: dextera, manus tua confregit inimicos.

ALLELUIA

Alleluia, alleluia. Corpora sanctorum in pace sepulta sunt, et nomina eorum vivent generationem et generationem. Alleluia.

Martyrs of Oxford University

Ps. 78: 1
Let the sighing of the prisoners come in before thee, O Lord; render to our neighbours sevenfold in their bosom; revenge the blood of thy saints, which hath been shed. V. O God, the heathens are come into thy inheritance: they have defiled thy holy temple: they have made Jerusalem as a place to keep fruit. Glory be.

O God, who for the defence of the true faith and of the authority of the Apostolic See, didst confirm thy blessed Martyrs Edmund and his Companions with invincible courage: do thou, moved by their prayers, we beseech thee, assist our weakness; that firm in faith, we may be enabled to withstand the enemy even unto the end. Through our Lord.

Apocalypse 7.13-17
At that time one of the ancients answered, and said to me: These that are clothed in white robes, who are they? and whence came they? And I said to him: My Lord, thou knowest. And he said to me: These are they who are come out of great tribulation, and have washed their robes, and have made them white in the blood of the Lamb. Therefore they are before the throne of God, and they serve him day and night in his temple: and he, that sitteth on the throne, shall dwell over them. They shall no more hunger nor thirst, neither shall the sun fall on them, nor any heat. For the Lamb, which is in the midst of the throne, shall rule them, and shall lead them to the fountains of the waters of life, and God shall wipe away all tears from their eyes.

Ex. 15:11,6
God is glorious in his Saints, wonderful in majesty, doing wonders. V. Thy right hand, O Lord, is glorified in strength; thy right hand hath broken the enemies.

Eccl. 44:14
Alleluia, alleluia. The bodies of the Saints are buried in peace, and their name liveth unto generation and generation. Alleluia.

GOSPEL

In illo tempore: Dixit Jesus discipulis suis: Cum audieritis prælia, et seditions, nolite terreri: Oportet Primum hæc fieri, sed nondum statim finis. Tunc dicebat illis : Surgeret gens contra gentem, et regnum adversus regnum. Et terræmotus magni erunt per loca, et pestilentiæ, et fames, terroresque de Cælo, et signa magna erunt. Sed ante hæc omnia injicient vobis manus suas, et presequentur tradentes in synagogas et custodias, trahentes ad reges et præsides propter nomen meum.: contingent autem vobis in testimonium. Ponite ergo in cordibus vestries non præmeditari quemadmodum respondeatis. Ego enim dabo vobis os, et sapientiam, cui non poterunt resistere, et contradicere omnes adversarii vestri. Trademini autem a parentibus, et fratribus, et cognates et amicis, et morte afficient ex vobis: et eritis odio omnibus propter nomen meum : et capillus de capite vestro non peribit. In Patientia vestra possidebitis animas vestras.

OFFERTORY

Mirabilis Deus in sanctis suis: Deus Israel, ipse dabit virtutem; et fortitudinem plebi : benedictus Deus.

SECRET

Sint tibi, Dómine, plebis tuæ múnera beatórum Mártyrum tuórum commemoratióne gratióra, nobísque fiant sancta oblatióne ac participatióne ad vitam ætérnam salutária. Per Dóminum nostrum.

Common Preface

COMMUNION

Et si coram hominibus tormenta passi eos: tamquuam aurum in furnace probavit eos, et quasi holocausta accepit eos.

POSTCOMMUNION

Domine Iesu Christe, quem in caritáte beatórum Mártyrum tuórum mirábilem prædicámus; da nobis, quæsumus, eórum précibus, ut in tua semper dilectióne maneámus: Qui vivis et regnas.

Luke 2.9-19

At that time, Jesus said to his disciples: When you shall hear of wars and seditions, be not terrified: these things must first come to pass, but the end is not yet presently. Then he said to them: Nation shall rise against nation, and kingdom against kingdom. And there shall be great earthquakes in divers places, and pestilences, and famines and terrors from heaven, and there shall be great signs. But before all these things, they will lay their hands on you and persecute you, delivering you up to the synagogues and into prisons, dragging you before kings and governors for my name's sake; and it shall happen unto you for a testimony. Lay it up therefore in your hearts, not to meditate before how you shall answer. For I will give you a mouth and wisdom, which all your adversaries shall not be able to resist and gainsay. And you shall be betrayed by your parents and brethren and kinsmen and friends, and some of you they will put to death : and you shall be hated by all men for my name's sake; but a hair of your head shall not perish. In your patience you shall possess your souls.

Ps. 67:36

God is wonderful in his saints: the God of Israel is he who will give power and strength.

May the offerings of thy people, O Lord, be made the more pleasing unto thee by the memory we make of thy blessed Martyrs: and may these gifts through this holy oblation and communion profit us unto life everlasting. Through our Lord.

Wis. 3:4, 6

And though in the sight of men they suffered torments, God hath tried them: as gold in the furnace he hath proved them, and as a victim of a holocaust he hath received them.

O Lord Jesus Christ, thou whom we declare to be wonderful in the love of thy blessed Martyrs, grant us, we beseech thee, through their prayers ever to abide in thy love: Who livest and reignest.

Missa Sanctæ Winefridæ

INTROIT

Me exspectavérunt peccatores, ut pérderent me: testimónia tua, Dómine, intelléxi: omnis consummatiónis vidi finem: latum mandátum tuum nimis. V. Beáti immaculáti in via: qui ámbulant in lege Dómini. Glória Patri.

COLLECT

Omnipotens sempitérne Deus, qui beátam Winefrídam virginitátis præmio donásti: fac nos, quæsumus, eius intercessióne mundi huius blandiménta postpónere, et cum ipsa perénnis glóriæ sedem obtínere. Per Dóminum

LECTION

Dómine, Deus meus, exaltásti super terram habitatiónem meam, et pro morre defluénte deprecáta sum. Invocávi Dóminum, Patrem Dómini mei, ut non derelínquat me in die tribulatiónis meæ, et in témpore superbórum sine adiutório. Laudábo nomen tuum assídue, et collaudábo illud in confessióne, et exaudíta est orátio mea. Et liberásti me de perditióne, et eripuísti me de témpore iníquo. Proptérea confitébor et laudem dicam tibi, Dómine, Deus noster.

GRADUAL

Adiuvábit eam Deus vultu suo: Deus in médio eius, non commovébitur. V. Flúminis ímpetus lætíficat civitátem Dei: sanctificávit tabernáculum suum Altíssimus.

ALLELUIA

Allelúia, allelúia. Hæc est Virgo sápiens, et una de número prudéntum. Allelúia.

GOSPEL

In illo témpore: Dixit Iesus discípulis suis parábolam hanc: Símile erit regnum cælórum decem virginibus: quæ, accipiéntes lámpades suas, exiérunt óbviam sponso et sponsæ. Quinque autem ex eis erant fátuæ, et quinque prudéntes: sed quinque fátuæ, accéptis lampádibus, non sumpsérunt oleum secum: prudéntes vero accepérunt

Mass of St Winefride

Ps 118:95-96
The wicked have waited for me to destroy me: but I have understood Thy testimonies, O Lord: I have seen an end of all perfection: Thy commandment is exceeding broad. V. Blessed are the undefiled in the way: who walk in the law of the Lord. Glory be.

O almighty, eternal God, who didst bestow on blessed Winefride the reward of virginity; grant us, we beseech thee, by her intercession to reject the alluring pleasures of the world, and to obtain with her a throne in everlasting glory. Through our Lord.

Eccl 51:13-17
O Lord my God, thou hast exalted my dwelling place upon the earth, and I have prayed for death to pass away. I called upon the Lord, the Father of my Lord, that he would not leave me in the day of my trouble, and in the time of the proud without help. I will praise Thy Name continually, and will praise it with thanksgiving, and my prayer was heard. And thou hast saved me from destruction, and hast delivered me from the evil time. Therefore I will give thanks and praise to thee, O Lord our God.

Ps 45:6; 45:5
God will help her with his countenance. God is in her midst; she shall not be disturbed. V. There is a stream whose runlets gladden the city of God; the Most High has sanctified his dwelling.

Alleluia, alleluia. This is a wise virgin, and one of the number of the prudent. Alleluia.

Matthew 25:1-13
At that time, Jesus spoke this parable to his disciples: Then will the kingdom of heaven be like ten virgins who took their lamps and went forth to meet the bridegroom and the bride. Five of them were foolish and five wise. But the five foolish, when they took their lamps, took no oil with them, while the wise did take oil in their vessels

óleum in vasis suis cum lampádibus. Moram autem
faciénte sponso, dormitavérunt omnes et dormiérunt.
Média autem nocte clamor factus est: Ecce, sponsus venit,
exíte óbviam ei. Tunc surrexérunt omnes vírgines illæ, et
ornavérunt lámpades suas. Fátuæ autem sapiéntibus
dixérunt: Date nobis de óleo vestro: quia lámpades nostræ
exstinguúntur. Respondérunt prudéntes, dicéntes: Ne forte
non suffíciat nobis et vobis, ite pótius ad vendéntes, et
émite vobis. Dum autem irent émere, venit sponsus: et
quæ parátæ erant, intravérunt cum eo ad núptias, et clausa
est iánua. Novíssime vero véniunt et réliquæ vírgines,
dicéntes: Dómine, Dómine, aperi nobis. At ille
respóndens, ait: Amen, dico vobis, néscio vos. Vigiláte
ítaque, quia nescítis diem neque horam.

OFFERTORY
Diffúsa est grátia in lábiis tuis: proptérea benedíxit te
Deus in ætérnum, et in sæculum sæculi.

SECRET
Hostias, Dómine, quas tibi offérimus, propítius réspice: et
intercédente beáta Winefrida, virgine tua et mártyre, vin-
cula peccatórum nostrórum absólve. Per Dominum nostrum Iesum Christum Filium tuum, qui tecum vivit et
regnat in unitate Spiritus Sancti, Deus, per ómnia sæcula
sæculórum. Amen.

Common Preface

COMMUNION
Feci iudícium et iustítiam, Dómine, non calumniéntur
mihi supérbi: ad ómnia mandáta tua dirigébar, omnem
viam iniquitátis ódio hábui.

POSTCOMMUNION
Placeant tibi, quæsumus,miséricors Deus, nostræ servitútis obséquia, ut mystéria sacrosáncta, quæ súmpsimus,
intercédente beáta Winefrida, Vírgine tua et Mártyre, et
tuam grátiam nobis concilient, et ætérnæ felicitátis gáudium subministrent. Per Dóminum.

70

with the lamps. Then as the bridegroom was long in coming, they all became drowsy and slept. And at midnight a cry arose and trimmed their lamps. And the foolish said to the wise, Give us some of your oil, for our lamps are going out. The wise answered, saying, Lest there may not be enough for us and for you, go rather to those who sell it, and buy some for yourselves. Now while they were gone to buy it, the bridegroom came; and those who were ready went in with him to the marriage feast, and the door was shut. Finally there came also the other virgins, who said, Sir, sir, open the door for us! But he answered and said, Amen I say to you, I do not know you. Watch therefore, for you know neither the day nor the hour.

Ps 44:3
Grace is poured out upon your lips; thus God has blessed you forever, and for ages of ages.

Favourably regard the offerings we make to thee, O Lord; and by the intercession of blessed Winefride, Thy virgin and martyr, set us free from the bonds of our sins. Through our Lord Jesus Christ, Thy Son, who liveth and reigneth with thee in the unity of the Holy Ghost, God, world without end. Amen.

Ps 118:121, 122, 128.
I have fulfilled just ordinances, O Lord; let not the proud oppress me. For in all thy precepts I go forward; every false way I hate.

May the homage of our service be pleasing unto thee, we beseech thee, O merciful God: that the most holy mysteries which we have received may, by the intercession of blessed Winefride, thy Virgin and Martyr, win us thy favour and procure for us the joy of eternal happiness. Through our Lord.

Missa Sancti Ricardi Gwyn

Lætábitur iustus in Dómino, et sperábit in eo: et laudabúntur omnes recticorde. V. Exáudi, Deus, oratiónem meam, cum déprecor: a timóre inimíci éripe ánimam meam. Gloria Patri.

Deus, qui beátum Ricárdum mártyrem tuum adolescéntium magístrum et cathólicæ fídei propugnatórem excitásti: concéde, quæsumus; ut nos in eádem fide eius exémplo roboráti, ad te perveníre felíciter valeámus. Per Dóminum.

Caríssime: Memor esto, Dóminum Iesum Christum resurrexísse a mórtuis ex sémine David, secúndum Evangélium meum, in quo labóro usque ad víncula, quasi male óperans: sed verbum Dei non est alligátum. Ideo ómnia sustíneo propter eléctos, ut et ipsi salútem consequántur, quæ est in Christo Iesu, cum glória cælésti. Tu autem assecútus es meam doctrínam, institutiónem, propósitum, fidem, longanimitátem, dilectiónem, patiéntiam, persecutiónes, passiónes: quália mihi facta sunt Antiochíæ, Icónii et Lystris: quales persecutiónes sustínui, et ex ómnibus erípuit me Dóminus. Et omnes, qui pie volunt vívere in Christo Iesu, persecutiónem patiéntur.

Iustus cum cecíderit, non collidétur: quia Dóminus suppónit manum suam. V. Tota die miserétur, et cómmodat: et semen eius in benedictióne erit.

Allelúia, allelúia. Qui séquitur me, non ámbulat in

Mass of St Richard Gwyn

Ps 63:11, 2
The just man is glad in the Lord and takes refuge in him;
all the upright of heart shall be praised. V. Hear, O God,
my voice in my lament; from the dread enemy preserve
my life. Glory be.

We implore thee, O God, who didst raise up Blessed
Richard to be an instructor of youth, a defender of the
Faith and thy martyr: so to strengthen us in that Faith by
his example, that we may in all joy finally come to thee.
Through our Lord.

2 Tim. 2:8 - 10; 3:10 - 12.
Beloved: Remember that Jesus Christ rose from the dead
and was descended from David; this is my Gospel, in
which I suffer even to bonds, as a criminal. But the word
of God is not bound. This is why I bear all things for the
sake of the elect, that they also may obtain the salvation
that is in Christ Jesus, with heavenly glory. But you have
closely followed my doctrine, my conduct, my purpose,
my faith, my long-suffering, my love, my patience, my
persecutions, my afflictions; such as befell me at Antioch,
Iconium and Lystra—such persecutions as I suffered, and
out of them all the Lord delivered me. And all who want
to live piously in Christ Jesus will suffer persecution.

Ps 36:24, 26.
Though the just man fall, he does not lie prostrate, for the
hand of the Lord sustains him. V. All the day he is kindly
and lends, and his descendants shall be blessed. Alleluia,
alleluia.

John 8:12
Alleluia, alleluia. He who follows me does not walk in

ténebris: sed habébit lumen vitæ ætérnæ. Allelúia.

In illo témpore: Dixit Iesus discípulis suis: Nihil est opértum, quod non revelábitur; et occúltum, quod non sciétur. Quod dico vobis in ténebris, dícite in lúmine: et quod in aure audítis, prædicáte super tecta. Et nolíte timére eos, qui occídunt corpus, ánimam autem non possunt occídere; sed pótius timéte eum, qui potest et ánimam et corpus pérdere in gehénnam. Nonne duo pásseres asse véneunt: et unus ex illis non cadet super terram sine Patre vestro? Vestri autem capílli cápitis omnes numerári sunt. Nolíte ergo timére: multis passéribus melióres estis vos. Omnis ergo, qui confitébitur me coram homínibus, confitébor et ego eum coram Patre meo, qui in cælis est.

Posuísti, Dómine, in cápite eius corónam de lápide pretióso: vitam pétiit a te, et tribuísti ei, allelúia.

Accépta sit in conspéctu tuo, Dómine, nostra devótio: et eius nobis fiat supplicatióne salutáris, pro cuius sollemnitáte defértur. Per Dominum

Common Preface

Qui mihi mínistrat, me sequátur: et ubi sum ego, illic et miníster meus erit.

Reféeti participatióne múneris sacri, quæsumus, Dómine, Deus noster: ut, cuius exséquimur cultum, intercedénte beáto Ricardo Mártyre tuo, sentiámus efféctum. Per Dominum.

darkness, but will have the light of life eternal. Alleluia.

Matt 10:26 - 32.
At that time, Jesus said to his disciples, There is nothing concealed that will not be disclosed, and nothing hidden that will not be made known. What I tell you in darkness, speak it in the light; and what you hear whispered, preach it on the housetops. And do not be afraid of those who kill the body but cannot kill the soul. But rather be afraid of him who is able to destroy both soul and body in hell. Are not two sparrows sold for a farthing? And yet not one of them will fall to the ground without your Father's leave. But as for you, the very hairs of your head are all numbered. Therefore do not be afraid; you are of more value than many sparrows. Therefore, everyone who acknowledges me before men, I also will acknowledge him before my Father in heaven.

Ps 20:4 - 5.
O Lord, thou hast placed on his head a crown of pure gold; he asked life of thee, and thou gavest it to him. Alleluia.

May our service be acceptable in thy sight, O Lord, and may it bring us salvation through the prayers of him on whose festival it is being offered. Through Our Lord.

John 12:26.
Whoever serves me, let him follow me; and where I am there also shall my servant be.

With our strength renewed from having shared in thy sacred gift, we beseech thee, O Lord our God, that by the intercession of blessed Richard, thy Martyr, we may feel the benefit of the worship we are offering. Through Our Lord.

75

Part II:
Public Devotions

Salutatio Angelica (*per annum*)

℣. Angelus Dómini nuntiávit Maríæ.

℟. Et concépit de Spíritu Sancto.

℣. Ave María, grátia plena, Dóminus tecum, benedícta tu in muliéribus, et benedíctus fructus ventris tui Iesus.

℟. Sancta María, Mater Dei, ora pro nobis peccatóribus, nunc et in hora mortis nostræ. Amen.

℣. Ecce ancílla Dómini:

℟. Fiat mihi secúndum verbum tuum.

> *Ave María...*

℣. Et Verbum caro factum est. (*kneel*)

℟. Et habitávit in nobis.

> *Ave María...*

℣. Ora pro nobis, Sancta Dei génetrix.

℟. Ut digni efficiámur promissiónibus Christi.

Orémus. Grátiam tuam, quæsumus, Dómine, méntibus nostris infúnde; ut qui, Ángelo nuntiánte, Christi Fílii tui incarnatiónem cognóvimus, per passiónem eius et crucem, ad resurrectiónis glóriam perducámur. Per eúndem Christum Dóminum nostrum.

℟. Amen.

Antiphona Mariana (*tempore Paschale*)

Omnes: Regína cæli, lætáre, allelúia. Quia quem meruísti portáre, allelúia. Resurréxit sicut dixit, allelúia. Ora pro nobis Deum, allelúia.

V. Gaude et lætáre, Virgo María, allelúia,

℟. Quia surréxit Dóminus vere, allelúia.

℣. Orémus.

Deus, qui per resurrectiónem Fílii tui, Dómini nostri, Iesu Christi, mundum lætificáre dignátus es: præsta, quæsumus, ut, per eius Genetrícem Vírginem Maríam, perpétuæ capiámus gáudia vitæ. Per eúndem Christum Dóminum nostrum.

℟. Amen.

THE ANGELUS (*outside Paschaltide*)

℣. The Angel of the Lord declared unto Mary:

℟. And she conceived of the Holy Ghost.

℣. Hail Mary, full of grace, the Lord is with thee; blessed art thou among women and blessed is the fruit of thy womb, Jesus.

℟. Holy Mary, Mother of God, pray for us sinners, now and at the hour of our death. Amen.

℟. Behold the handmaid of the Lord:

R. Be it done unto me according to thy word.

> *Hail Mary...*

℣. And the word was made flesh: (*kneel*)

℟. And dwelt amongst us.

> *Hail Mary...*

℣. Pray for us, O Holy Mother of God.

℟. That we may be made worthy of the promises of Christ.

Let us pray: Pour forth, we beseech thee, O Lord, thy grace into our hearts; that we, to whom the Incarnation of Christ, thy Son, was made known by the message of an angel, may be brought, by his Passion and Cross, to the glory of his Resurrection, through the same Christ our Lord.

℟. Amen.

REGINA CÆLI (*during Paschaltide*)

All: O Queen of Heaven rejoice, alleluia: For he whom thou didst merit to bear, alleluia, has risen as he said, alleluia. Pray for us to God, alleluia.

℣. Rejoice and be glad, O Virgin Mary, alleluia.

℟. For the Lord has risen indeed, alleluia.

℣. Let us pray.

O God, who gavest joy to the world through the Resurrection of thy Son our Lord Jesus Christ: grant we may obtain, through his Virgin Mother, Mary, the joys of everlasting life. Through the same Christ our Lord.

℟. Amen.

Ad Benedictionem SS. Sacramenti

(for chants see pp88ff)

O Salutáris Hóstia
Quæ cæli pandis óstium
Bella premunt hostília;
Da robur, fer auxílium.

Uni trinóque Dómino,
Sit sempitérna glória;
Qui vitam sine término,
Nobis donet in pátria. Amen.

Prayer for England (Prayer for Scotland: p87)

O beáta Virgo María, Mater Dei, Regína nostra et Mater dulcíssima, benígna óculos tuos convérte ad Ángliam, quæ Dos tua vocátur, convérte ad nos, qui magna in te fidúcia confídimus.

Per te datus est Christus Salvátor mundi, in quo spes nostra consísteret; ab ipso autem tu data es nobis, per quam spes éadem augerétur. Eia ígitur, ora pro nobis, quos tibi apud Crucem Dómini excepísti fílios, o pérdolens Mater: intercéde pro frátribus dissidéntibus, ut nobíscum in único vero Ovíli adiungántur summo Pastóri, Vicário in terris Fílii tui.

Pro nobis ómnibus deprecáre, o Mater piíssima, ut per fidem, bonis opéribus fecúndam, mereámur tecum omnes contemplári Deum in cælésti pátria et collaudáre per sǽcula.
℞. Amen.

Gweddi dros Gymru

O Hollalluog Dduw a ddanfonodd, o'th anfeidrol ddaioni, dy unig-anedig Fab i ailagor porth y nefoedd, ac i ddysgu inni dy adnabod, dy garu a'th wasnaethu, trugarha wrth

BENEDICTION OF THE BLESSED SACRAMENT
(for chants see pp88ff)

O Saving Victim, thou who dost throw open heaven's gate, the enemy's wars press hard on us; give us strength, bring us help.

Everlasting glory be to the Lord, one and three; and may he give us unending life in our Father's land. Amen.

PRAYER FOR ENGLAND (Prayer for Scotland: p87)

O Blessed Virgin Mary, Mother of God and our most gentle Queen and Mother, look down in mercy upon England, thy dowry, and upon us who greatly hope and trust in thee.

By thee it was that Jesus, our Saviour and our hope was given unto the world; and he has given thee to us that we might hope still more.

Plead for us thy children, whom thou didst receive and accept at the foot of the Cross, O sorrowful Mother! Intercede for our separated brethren, that with us in the one true fold they may be united to the chief Shepherd, the Vicar of thy Son.

Pray for us all, dear Mother, that by faith fruitful in good works, we may all deserve to see and praise God, together with thee, in our heavenly home.
℟. Amen.

PRAYER FOR WALES

O Almighty God, who in thy infinite goodness hast sent thy only-begotten Son into this world to open once more the gates of heaven, and to teach us

dy bobl sy'n byw yng Nghymru. Dyro iddynt y werthfawr ddawn Ffydd, ac una hwy yn yr un wir Eglwys a sylfaenwyd gan dy ddwyfol Fab, fel, gan arddel ei hawdurdod a chan ufuddhau i'w llais, y'th wasnaethont Di, a'th garu a'th addoli yn ôl dy ewyllys yn y byd hwn, ac felly dderbyn ohonynt ddedwyddwch tragwyddol yn y byd a ddaw. Trwy'r un Iesu Grist ein Harglwydd.

℟. Amen.
℣. Ein Harglwyddes, Gymorth Cristnogion,
℟. gweddïa dros Gymru.
℣. Dewi Sant,
℟. gweddïa dros Gymru.
℣. Santes Wenfrewi,
℟. gweddïa dros Gymru.

> Tantum ergo sacraméntum,
> Venerémur cérnui;
> Et antíquum documéntum
> Novo cedat rítui;
> Præstet fides suppleméntum
> Sénsuum deféctui.
>
> Genitóri, Genitóque,
> Laus et iubilátio
> Salus, honor, virtus quoque
> Sit et benedíctio
> Procedénti ab utróque
> Compar sit laudátio. Amen.

℣. Panem de cælo præstitísti eis (Allelúia).
℟. Omne delectaméntum in se habéntem (Allelúia).

P: Orémus: Deus, qui nobis, sub sacraménto mirábili, passiónis tuæ memóriam reliquísti, tríbue quæsumus, ita nos córporis et sánguinis tui sacra mystéria venerári, ut redemptiónis tui fructum in nobis iúgiter sentiámus. Qui vivis et regnas in sæcula sæculórum.
℟. Amen.

how to know, love and serve thee, have mercy on thy people who dwell in Wales. Grant to them the precious gift of faith, and unite them in the one true Church founded by thy divine Son; that, acknowledging her authority and obeying her voice, they may serve thee, love thee, and worship thee as thou desirest in this world, and obtain for themselves everlasting happiness in the world to come. Through the same Christ our Lord.

℞. Amen.

℣. Our Lady, Help of Christians,

℞. pray for Wales.

℣. Saint David,

℞. pray for Wales.

℣. Saint Winifride,

℞. pray for Wales.

Let us therefore humbly reverence so great a sacrament. Let the old types depart and give way to the new rite. Let faith provide her help where all the senses fail.

To the Father and the Son be praise, acclamation, salutation, honour, might and blessing too. To the One who proceeds from them both be given equal praise. Amen

℣. Thou hast given them bread from heaven (Alleluia).

℞. Having in it all that is delicious (Alleluia).

P. Let us pray: O God, who in this wonderful Sacrament hast left us a memorial of thy passion: grant us, we pray, so to revere the sacred mysteries of thy Body and Blood, that we may always experience in ourselves the fruit of thy redemption. Who livest and reignest forever and ever.

℞. Amen.

Parce, Dómine, parce pópulo tuo, et ne in ætérnam irascáris nobis. *(Ter)*

The Priest, wearing the humeral veil, blesses the Faithful with the Blessed Sacrament.

Benedíctus Deus.
Benedíctum Nomen Sanctum eius.
Benedíctus Iesus Christus, verus Deus et verus homo.
Benedíctum Nomen Iesu.
Benedíctum Cor eius sacratíssimum.
Benedíctus Sanguis eius pretiosíssimus.
Benedíctus Iesus in sanctíssimo altáris Sacraménto.
Benedíctus Sanctus Spíritus, Paráclitus.
Benedícta magna Mater Dei, María sanctíssima.
Benedícta sancta eius et immaculáta Concéptio.
Benedícta gloriósa eius Assúmptio.
Benedíctum nomen Maríæ, Vírginis et Matris.
Benedíctus sanctus Ioseph, eius castíssimus Sponsus.
Benedíctus Deus in Angelis suis et in Sanctis suis.

Antiphon: Adorémus in ætérnum sanctíssimum Sacraméntum.

Laudáte Dóminum omnes gentes: * laudáte eum omnes pópuli.
Quóniam confirmáta est super nos misericórdia eius: *
        et véritas Dómini manet in ætérnum.

Antiphon: Adorémus in ætérnum sanctíssimum Sacraméntum.

Glória Patri, et Fílio, et Spirítui Sancto: Sicut erat in princípio, et nunc et semper, et in sǽcula sæculórum. Amen.

Antiphon: Adorémus in ætérnum sanctíssimum Sacraméntum.

Spare, O Lord, spare thy people, and be not angry with them for ever. (*Thrice*)

The Priest, wearing the humeral veil, blesses the Faithful with the Blessed Sacrament.

Blessed be God.
Blessed be his holy Name.
Blessed be Jesus Christ, true God and true man.
Blessed be the name of Jesus.
Blessed be his most sacred Heart.
Blessed be his most precious Blood.
Blessed be Jesus in the most holy Sacrament of the Altar.
Blessed be the Holy Ghost, the Paraclete.
Blessed be the great Mother of God, Mary most holy.
Blessed be her holy and immaculate Conception.
Blessed be her glorious Assumption.
Blessed be the name of Mary, virgin and mother.
Blessed be St Joseph, her spouse most chaste.
Blessed be God in his Angels and in his Saints.

Antiphon: Let us adore for ever the most holy Sacrament.

Praise the Lord, all ye nations: * praise him all ye peoples.
Because his mercy is confirmed upon us: *
and the truth of the Lord remains forever.

Antiphon: Let us adore for ever the most holy Sacrament.

Glory be to the Father, and to the Son, and to the Holy Ghost: as it was in the beginning, is now, and ever shall be, world without end. Amen.

Antiphon: Let us adore for ever the most holy Sacrament.

LONG PRAYER FOR ENGLAND
mandated by Cardinal Wiseman for Benediction on the Second Sundays.

Hail Mary, etc.

O merciful God, let the glorious intercession of thy
saints assist us; above all the most blessed Virgin Mary,
Mother of thy only-begotten Son, and thy holy Apostles,
Peter and Paul, to whose patronage we humbly recom-
mend our land. Be mindful of our fathers, Eleutherius,
Celestine and Gregory, bishops of the holy City; of Augustine, Columba, and Aidan, who delivered to us invio-
late the faith of the holy Roman Church. Remember our
holy martyrs, who shed their blood for Christ; especially
our first martyr, Saint Alban, and thy most glorious bishop, Saint Thomas of Canterbury. Remember all those
holy confessors, bishops and kings, all those holy monks
and hermits, all those holy virgins and widows, who
made this once an island of saints, illustrious by their
glorious merits and virtues. Let not their memory perish
from before thee, O Lord, but let their supplication enter
daily into thy sight; and do thou, who didst so often
spare thy sinful people for the sake of Abraham, Isaac
and Jacob, now, also, moved by the prayers of our fathers, reigning with thee, have mercy upon us, save thy
people, and bless thy inheritance; and suffer not those
souls to perish, which thy Son has redeemed with his
own most precious Blood. Who liveth and reigneth with
thee, world without end.

℟. Amen.

Let us pray. O loving Lord Jesus, who, when thou wert
hanging on the Cross, didst commend us all, in the person of thy disciple John, to thy most sweet Mother, that
we might find in her our refuge, our solace, and our
hope; look graciously upon our beloved land, and on
those who are bereaved of so powerful a patronage; that,
acknowledging once more the dignity of this holy Virgin, they may honour and venerate her with all affection
of devotion, and own her as Queen and Mother. May her
sweet name be lisped by little ones, and linger on the lips

of the aged and the dying; and may it be invoked by the afflicted, and hymned by the joyful; that this Star of the Sea being their protection and their guide, all may come to the harbour of eternal salvation. Who livest and reignest, world without end.

℞. Amen.

PRAYER FOR SCOTLAND

O blessed St Andrew, First-Called and Fisher of men, of old thou didst summon thy brother St Peter into the presence of the Saviour; obtain now, we beseech thee, by thy powerful intercession for the people of Scotland that they might recognise in his successor the Vicar of Christ, and so enter into the vision of him who with the Father and the Holy Ghost lives and reigns, one God, for ever and ever. Amen.

GRACE BEFORE MEALS

Bénedic, Dómine, nos et hæc tua dona quæ de tua largitáte sumus sumptúri. Per Christum Dóminum nostrum. Amen.

THANKSGIVING AFTER MEALS

Ágimus tibi grátias, omnípotens Deus, pro univérsis benefíciis tuis, qui vivis et regnas in sǽcula sæculórum. Amen.

Fidélium ánimæ, per misericórdiam Dei, requiéscant in pace. Amen.

Chants for Benediction

O SALUTARIS HOSTIA

Hymn. VIII.

O Sa- lu- tá-ris Hósti- a, Quæ cǽ-li pandis ó- sti- um: Bella premunt hostí- li- a, Da ro-bur, fer auxí-li- um. 2. Uni tri-nó-que Dómino Sit sempi-térna gló- ri- a, Qui vi-tam si- ne término Nobis donet in pátri- a. Amen.

TANTUM ERGO

Hymn. III.

T Antum ergo Sacraméntum Venerémur cérnu- i: Et antíquum documéntum Novo cedat rí-tu- i: Præstet fi-des suppleméntum Sénsu- um de-féctu- i. 6. Geni-tóri, Geni- tóque Laus et iubi-lá-ti- o, Salus, honor, virtus quoque Sit et be-nedícti- o: Proce-dénti ab utróque Compar sit laudá- ti- o Amen.

LAUDES DIVINÆ
The Divine Praises

Bene-dictus De- us. * Benedictum Nomen Sanctum e- ius.

Benedictus Iesus Christus, * verus De-us et ve-rus homo.

Bene-dictum Nomen Ie-su. * Bene-dictum Cor eius sacra

tissi-mum.

Bene-dictus e- ius * Sanguis pre- ti- o- sissimum.

Bene-dictus Iesus * in sanctissimo altaris Sacramento.

Bene-dictus Sanctus * Spi-ri- tus, Pa-racli- tus.

Bene-dicta magna Mater De- i, * Mari- a sanctissi-ma.

Bene-dicta sancta e- ius * Et immacu-la-ta Con-cepti- o.

Bene-dicta e- ius * glori- o-sa Assumpti- o.

Bene-dictum nomen Ma-ri- ae, * Virgi-nis et Matris.

Benedictus sanctus Io-seph, * Eius castis-si-mus Sponsus.

Benedictus De-us in Ange-lis su-is, * Et in Sanctis su-is.

Fi-at Fi-at

ADOREMUS

Adorémus in ætérnum sanctíssimum Sacraméntum.

Ps. Laudá-te Dóminum omnes gentes: * laudá-te e-um omnes

pópu-li. Quóni-am confirmá-ta est super nos mi-sericórdi-a

e-ius: * et vé-ritas Dómini manet in ætérnum. Adorémus.

Gló-ri-a Patri et Fí-li-o, * et Spi-rí-tu-i Sancto. Sicut erat

in princí-pi-o, et nunc, et semper: et in sǽcu-la sæcu-ló-

rum. Amen. Adorémus.

STATIONS OF THE CROSS
From the *Manual of Prayers* (1953)

The Priest and Acolytes, kneeling before the altar, say as follows:

O JESUS, our adorable Saviour, behold us prostrate at thy feet, imploring thy mercy for ourselves, and for the souls of all the faithful departed. Vouchsafe to apply to us the infinite merits of thy Passion, on which we are now about to meditate. Grant that while we trace this path of sighs and tears, our hearts may be so touched with contrition and repentance, that we may be ready to embrace with joy all the crosses, sufferings, and humiliations of this our life and pilgrimage.

℣. Thou shalt open my lips, O Lord.
℟. And my mouth shall show forth thy praise.
℣. O God, come to my assistance.
℟. O Lord, make haste to help me.
℣. Glory be to the Father, *etc.*
℟. As it was in the beginning, *etc.*

Then the Priest and people move in procession to the First Station.

FIRST STATION
JESUS IS CONDEMNED TO DEATH

℣. We adore thee, O Christ, and we bless thee.
℟. Because by thy holy Cross thou hast redeemed the world.

Leaving the house of Caiaphas, where he had been blasphemed, and the house of Herod, where he had been mocked, Jesus is dragged before Pilate, his back torn with scourges, his head crowned with thorns; and he, who on the last day will judge the living and the dead, is himself condemned to a disgraceful death.

IT was for us that thou didst suffer, O blessed Jesus; it was for our sins thou wast condemned to die. Oh, grant that we may detest them from the bottom of our hearts, and by this repentance obtain thy mercy and pardon.

AN ACT OF CONTRITION

O GOD, we love thee with our whole hearts and above all things, and are heartily sorry that we have offended thee. May we never offend thee any more. Oh, may we love thee without ceasing, and make it our delight to do in all things thy most holy will.

Our Father. Hail Mary. Glory be to the Father.

Have mercy on us, O Lord; have mercy on us.

℣. May the souls of the faithful departed, through the mercy of God, rest in peace.
℟. Amen.

This Act of Contrition is to be repeated after each Station. While passing from one Station to another, a verse of the STABAT MATER is sung or said.

℣. Stabat Mater dolorósa, Iuxta crucem lacrymósa,
    Dum pendébat Fílius.

Dum pendébat Fí-li-us.

℟. Sancta Mater, istud agas, Crucifixi fige plagas
    Cordi meo válide.

SECOND STATION
JESUS RECEIVES THE CROSS

℣. We adore thee, O Christ, and we bless thee.
℟. Because by thy holy Cross thou hast redeemed the world.

A heavy cross is laid upon the bruised shoulders of Jesus. He receives it with meekness, nay, with a secret joy, for it is the instrument with which he is to redeem the world.
O JESUS! grant us, by virtue of thy cross, to embrace with meekness and cheerful submission the difficulties of our state, and to be ever ready to take up our cross and follow thee.

Act of Contrition, etc., as before.

℣. Cujus ánimam geméntem, Contristátam, et doléntem,
     Pertransívit gládius.
℟. Sancta Mater, istud agas, Crucifíxi fige plagas
     Cordi meo válide.

THIRD STATION
JESUS FALLS THE FIRST TIME UNDER HIS CROSS

℣. We adore thee, O Christ, and we bless thee.
℟. Because by thy holy Cross thou hast redeemed the world.

Bowed down under the weight of the cross, Jesus slowly sets forth on the way to Calvary, amidst the mockeries and insults of the crowd. His agony in the garden has exhausted his body; he is sore with blows and wounds; his strength fails him; he falls to the ground under the cross.

O JESUS! who for our sins didst bear the heavy burden of the cross, and fell under its weight, may the thoughts of thy sufferings make us watchful over ourselves, and save us from any grievous fall into sin.

Act of Contrition, etc., as before.

℣. O quam tristis et afflícta, Fuit illa benedícta
      Mater Unigéniti!
℟. Sancta Mater, istud agas, Crucifíxi fige plagas
      Cordi meo válide.

FOURTH STATION
JESUS IS MET BY HIS BLESSED MOTHER

℣. We adore thee, O Christ, and we bless thee.
℟. Because by thy holy Cross thou hast redeemed the world.

Still burdened with his cross, and wounded yet more by his fall, Jesus proceeds on his way. He is met by his Mother. What a meeting must that have been! What a sword of anguish must have pierced that Mother's bosom! What must have been the compassion of that Son for his holy Mother!

O JESUS! by the compassion which thou didst feel for thy Mother, have compassion on us, and give us a share in her intercession. O Mary, most afflicted Mother! intercede for us that, through the sufferings of thy Son, we may be delivered from the wrath to come.

Act of Contrition, etc., as before.

℣. Quæ mœrébat et dolébat, Pia Mater, dum vidébat
      Nati pœnas ínclyti.
℟. Sancta Mater, istud agas, Crucifíxi fige plagas
      Cordi meo válide.

FIFTH STATION
THE CROSS IS LAID UPON SIMON OF CYRENE

℣. We adore thee, O Christ, and we bless thee.
℟. Because by thy holy Cross thou hast redeemed the world.

94

As the strength of Jesus fails, and he is unable to proceed, the executioners seize and compel Simon of Cyrene to carry his cross. The virtue of that cross changed his heart, and from a compulsory task it became a privilege and a joy.

O LORD Jesus! may it be our privilege also to bear thy cross; may we glory in nothing else; by it may the world be crucified unto us, and we unto the world; may we never shrink from sufferings, but rather rejoice if we may be counted worthy to suffer for thy name's sake.

Act of Contrition, etc., as before.

℣. Quis est homo qui non fleret,
   Matrem Christi si vidéret, In tanto supplício?
℟. Sancta Mater, istud agas, Crucifixi fige plagas
   Cordi meo válide.

SIXTH STATION
VERONICA WIPES THE FACE OF JESUS

℣ We adore thee, O Christ, and we bless thee.
℟ Because by thy holy Cross thou hast redeemed the world.

As Jesus proceeds on the way, covered with the sweat of death, a woman, moved with compassion, makes her way through the crowd, and wipes his face with a towel upon which, as a reward of her piety, the impression of his sacred countenance is miraculously imprinted.

O JESUS! may the contemplation of thy sufferings move us with the deepest compassion, make us to hate our sins, and kindle in our hearts more fervent love to thee. May thy image be graven on our minds, until we are transformed into thy likeness.

Act of Contrition, etc., as before.

℣. Quis non posset contristári,
        Christi Matrem contemplári, Doléntem cum Fílio?
℟. Sancta Mater, istud agas, Crucifíxi fige plagas
        Cordi meo válide.

SEVENTH STATION
JESUS FALLS THE SECOND TIME

℣. We adore thee, O Christ, and we bless thee.
℟. Because by thy holy Cross thou hast redeemed the world.

The pain of his wounds and the loss of blood increasing at every step of his way, again his strength fails him, and Jesus falls to the ground a second time.

O JESUS! falling again under the burden of our sins, and of thy sufferings for our sins, how often have we grieved thee by our repeated falls into sin! Oh, may we rather die than ever offend thee again!

Act of Contrition, etc., as before.

℣. Pro peccátis suæ gentis, Vidit Iesum in torméntis,
        Et flagéllis súbditum.
℟. Sancta Mater, istud agas, Crucifíxi fige plagas
        Cordi meo válide.

EIGHTH STATION
THE WOMEN OF JERUSALEM MOURN
FOR OUR LORD

℣. We adore thee, O Christ, and we bless thee.
℟. Because by thy holy Cross thou hast redeemed the world.

At the sight of the sufferings of Jesus some holy women in the crowd were so touched with sympathy that they openly bewailed and lamented him. Jesus knowing the things that were to come to pass upon Jerusalem because of its rejection of him, turned to them and said, "Daughters of Jerusalem, weep not for me, but weep for yourselves and for your children."

O LORD Jesus, we mourn, and will always mourn, both for thee and for ourselves; for thy sufferings and for our sins which caused them. Oh, teach us so to mourn, that we may be comforted, and escape those dreadful judgements prepared for all who reject or neglect thee in this life.

Act of Contrition, etc., as before.

℣. Vidit suum dulcem Natum, Moriéndo desolátum,
     Dum emísit spíritum.
℟. Sancta Mater, istud agas, Crucifíxi fige plagas
     Cordi meo válide.

NINTH STATION
JESUS FALLS THE THIRD TIME

℣. We adore thee, O Christ, and we bless thee.
℟. Because by thy holy Cross thou hast redeemed the world.

Jesus had now arrived almost at the summit of Calvary; but before he reached the spot where he was to be crucified, his strength again fails him, and he falls the third time, to be again dragged up and goaded onward by the brutal soldiers.

O LORD Jesus! we entreat thee, by the merits of this thy third most painful fall, to pardon our frequent relapses and our long continuance in sin; and may the thought of these thy sufferings make us to hate our sins more and more.

Act of Contrition, etc., as before.

℣. Eia, Mater, fons amóris, Me sentíre vim dolóris,
    Fac, ut tecum lúgeam.
℟. Sancta Mater, istud agas, Crucifíxi fige plagas
    Cordi meo válide.

TENTH STATION
JESUS IS STRIPPED OF HIS GARMENTS

℣. We adore thee, O Christ, and we bless thee.
℟. Because by thy holy Cross thou hast redeemed the world.

Arrived at last at the place of sacrifice, they prepare to crucify him. His garments are torn from his bleeding body, and he, the Holy of Holies, stands exposed to the vulgar gaze of the rude and scoffing multitude.
O LORD Jesus, thou didst endure this shame for our most shameful deeds. Strip us, we beseech thee, of all false shame and pride, and make us so to humble ourselves in this life, that we may escape everlasting ignominy in the world to come.

Act of Contrition, etc., as before.

℣. Fac, ut árdeat cor meum, In amándo Christum Deum,
    Ut sibi compláceam.
℟. Sancta Mater, istud agas, Crucifíxi fige plagas
    Cordi meo válide.

ELEVENTH STATION
JESUS IS NAILED TO THE CROSS

℣. We adore thee, O Christ, and we bless thee.
℟. Because by thy holy Cross thou hast redeemed the world.

The cross is laid upon the ground, and Jesus is stretched upon his bed of death. He offers his bruised limbs to his heavenly Father on behalf of sinful man, and to his fierce executioners to be nailed by them to the disgraceful wood. The blows are struck! The blood gushes forth!

O JESUS, nailed to the cross, fasten our hearts there also, that they may be united to thee until death shall strike us, and with our last breath we shall have yielded up our souls to thee.

Act of Contrition, etc., as before.

℣. Sancta Mater, istud agas; Crucifíxi fige plagas,
　　　Cordi meo válide.
℟. Sancta Mater, istud agas, Crucifíxi fige plagas
　　　Cordi meo válide.

TWELFTH STATION
JESUS DIES ON THE CROSS

℣. We adore thee, O Christ, and we bless thee.
℟. Because by thy holy Cross thou hast redeemed the world.

For three hours Jesus has hung upon his transfixed hands; his blood has run in streams down his body, and bedewed the ground; and, in the midst of excruciating sufferings, he has pardoned his murderers, promised the bliss of paradise to the good thief, and committed his blessed Mother and beloved disciple to each other's care. All is now consummated; and meekly bowing down his head, he gives up the ghost.

O JESUS! we embrace devoutly that honoured cross whereon thou didst love us even unto death. In that death we place all our confidence. Henceforth let us live only for thee; and when we die, let us die loving thee, and in thy sacred arms.

Act of Contrition, etc., as before.

℣. Tui Nati vulneráti, Tam dignáti pro me pati,
　　　Pœnas mecum dívide.

℟. Sancta Mater, istud agas, Crucifíxi fige plagas
      Cordi meo válide.

THIRTEENTH STATION
JESUS IS TAKEN DOWN FROM THE CROSS

℣. We adore thee, O Christ, and we bless thee.
℟. Because by thy holy Cross thou hast redeemed the world.

The multitude have left the heights of Calvary, and none remain save the beloved disciple and the holy women, who, at the foot of the cross, are sharing the grief of Christ's holy Mother. Joseph of Arimathea and Nicodemus take down the body of her divine Son from the cross and lay it in her arms.

O THOU, whose grief was boundless as an ocean, Mary, Mother of God, give us a share in thy most holy sorrow for the sufferings of thy Son, and have compassion on our infirmities. Accept us as thy children with the beloved disciple. Show thyself a mother unto us; and may he, through thee, receive our prayer, who for us vouchsafed to be thy Son.

Act of Contrition, etc., as before.

℣. Fac me tecum pie flere, Crucifíxo condoláre,
      Donec ego víxero.
℟. Sancta Mater, istud agas, Crucifíxi fige plagas
      Cordi meo válide.

FOURTEENTH STATION
JESUS IS LAID IN THE SEPULCHRE

℣. We adore thee, O Christ, and we bless thee.
℟. Because by thy holy Cross thou hast redeemed the world.

The body of her dearly beloved Son is taken from his Mother, and laid by the disciples in the tomb. The tomb is closed, and there Christ's sacred body remains until the hour of its glorious resurrection.

WE, too, O God, will descend into the grave whenever it shall please thee, as it shall please thee, and wheresoever it shall please thee. Let thy just decrees be fulfilled; let our sinful bodies return to their parent dust, but do thou, in thy great mercy, receive our immortal souls, and when our bodies have risen again, place them likewise in thy kingdom that we may love and bless thee for ever and ever. Amen.

Act of Contrition, etc., as before.

℣. Juxta crucem tecum stare, Et me tibi sociáre,
    In planctu desídero.
℞. Sancta Mater, istud agas, Crucifíxi fige plagas
    Cordi meo válide.

LATIN AND ENGLISH ROSARY PRAYERS

ENGLISH (half-way points indicated by *)
Sign of the Cross
In the name of the Father, and of the Son, and of the Holy
Ghost.

Apostles Creed
I believe in God, the Father Almighty, Creator of Heaven
and earth; and in Jesus Christ, his only Son Our Lord,
Who was conceived by the Holy Ghost, born of the Virgin Mary, suffered under Pontius Pilate, was crucified,
died, and was buried. He descended into Hell; on the
third day he rose again from the dead; he ascended into
Heaven, sitteth at the right hand of God, the Father
almighty; from thence he shall come to judge the living
and the dead. * **I believe in the Holy Ghost, the holy
Catholic Church, the communion of saints, the forgiveness of sins, the resurrection of the body and life
everlasting. Amen.**

Our Father
Our Father, who art in heaven, hallowed be thy name.
Thy Kingdom come. Thy will be done, on earth as it is in
Heaven. * **Give us this day our daily bread. And forgive us our trespasses, as we forgive those who trespass against us. And lead us not into temptation, but
deliver us from evil. Amen.**

Hail Mary
Hail Mary, full of grace, the Lord is with thee. Blessed
art thou among women, and blessed is the fruit of thy
womb, Jesus. * **Holy Mary, Mother of God, pray for
us sinners now, and at the hour of our death. Amen.**

LATIN AND ENGLISH ROSARY PRAYERS

LATIN
Signum Crucis
In nómine Patris, et Fílii, et Spíritus Sancti. Amen.

Symbólum Apostolórum
Credo in Deum Patrem omnipoténtem, Creatórem cæli et terræ. Et in Iesum Christum, Fílium eius únicum, Dóminum nostrum, qui concéptus est de Spíritu Sancto, natus ex María Vírgine, passus sub Póntio Piláto, crucifíxus, mórtuus, et sepúltus: descéndit ad ínferos; tértia die resurréxit a mórtuis; ascéndit ad cælos; sedet ad déxteram Dei Patris omnipoténtis: inde ventúrus est iudicáre vivos et mórtuos. Credo in Spíritum Sanctum, sanctam Ecclésiam cathólicam, Sanctórum communiónem, remissiónem peccatórum, carnis resurrectiónem, vitam ætérnam. Amen.

Pater Noster
Pater noster, qui es in cælis: Sanctificétur nomen tuum: Advéniat regnum tuum: Fiat volúntas tua, sicut in cælo, et in terra. Panem nostrum cotidiánum da nobis hódie: et dimítte nobis débita nostra, sicut et nos dimíttimus debitóribus nostris. Et ne nos indúcas in tentatiónem. Sed líbera nos a malo. Amen.

Salutátio Angélica
Ave, María, grátia plena; Dóminus tecum: benedícta tu in muliéribus, et benedíctus fructus ventris tui, Iesus. Sancta María, Mater Dei, ora pro nobis peccatóribus, nunc et in hora mortis nostræ. Amen.

Glory Be (Lesser Doxology)
Glory be to the Father, and to the Son, and to the Holy Ghost. *** As it was in the beginning, is now, and ever shall be, world without end. Amen.**

Fatima Prayer
O my Jesus, forgive us our sins, save us from the fires of hell, and lead all souls to heaven, especially those in most need of thy mercy. Amen.

Hail Holy Queen
Hail Holy Queen, mother of mercy; hail our life, our sweetness, and our hope. To thee do we cry, poor banished children of Eve. To thee do we send up our sighs, mourning and weeping in this vale of tears. Turn, then, most gracious advocate, thine eyes of mercy toward us. And after this, our exile, show unto us the blessed fruit of thy womb, Jesus. O clement, O loving, O sweet Virgin Mary.

℣. Pray for us, O holy Mother of God.

℟. That we may be made worthy of the promises of Christ.

Let us pray. O God, whose only-begotten Son by his life, death and resurrection, has purchased for us the rewards of eternal life; grant, we beseech thee, that by meditating upon these mysteries of the Most Holy Rosary of the Blessed Virgin Mary, we may imitate what they contain and obtain what they promise, through Christ our Lord. Amen.

Glória Patri (Doxológia Minor)

Glória Patri, et Fílio, et Spirítui Sancto. Sicut erat in princípio, et nunc, et semper, et in sǽcula sæculórum. Amen.

Oratio Fatimæ

Dómine Iesu, dimítte nobis débita nostra, salva nos ab igne inferióri, perdúc in cælum omnes ánimas, præsértim eas, quæ misericórdiæ tuæ máxime índigent.

Salve Regína

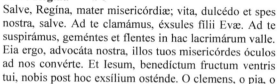

Salve, Regína, mater misericórdiæ; vita, dulcédo et spes nostra, salve. Ad te clamámus, éxsules fílii Evæ. Ad te suspirámus, geméntes et flentes in hac lacrimárum valle. Eia ergo, advocáta nostra, illos tuos misericórdes óculos ad nos convérte. Et Iesum, benedíctum fructum ventris tui, nobis post hoc exsílium osténde. O clemens, o pia, o dulcis Virgo María.

℣. Ora pro nobis, Sancta Dei Génetrix.
℟. Ut digni efficiámur promissiónibus Christi.

Orémus: Deus, cuius Unigénitus per vitam, mortem et resurrectiónem suam nobis salútis ætérnæ præmia comparávit: concéde, quǽsumus; ut, hæc mystéria sacratíssimo beátæ Maríæ Virginis Rosário recoléntes, et imitémur, quod cóntinent, et quod promíttunt, assequámur. Per eúndem Christum Dóminum nostrum. Amen.

SETTINGS OF THE HAIL MARY

Hail Mary, full of grace. The
Lord is with thee. Blessed are thou among women, and blessed is the fruit of thy womb, Jesus. Holy Mary, Mother of God, pray for us sinners, now and at the hour of our death. Amen.

Fr Bede Rowe

106

MEDITATIONS ON THE ROSARY OF THE BLESSED VIRGIN MARY

From the *Manual of Prayers* (1953)

The fifteen mysteries are divided into three parts, viz. five JOYFUL, five SORROWFUL, and five GLORIOUS mysteries. We should endeavour to arouse corresponding affections in the will during the recital of each Decade, such as the devotion of each one may suggest; for example, in the first part, sentiments of joy for the coming of our Redeemer; in the second, of compassion for the sufferings of our Lord, and contrition for our sins, which were the occasion of them; in the third, of thanksgiving for the exaltation and glory of our Saviour and of his Blessed Mother, hoping, through the merits of his Passion and by her intercession, to be made partakers of their glory.

THE JOYFUL MYSTERIES

Usually recited on Mondays and Thursdays throughout the year, and the Sundays from Advent to Quinquagesima.

I. THE ANNUNCIATION

Let us contemplate in this mystery, how the angel Gabriel saluted our Blessed Lady with the title, "full of grace," and declared to her the incarnation of our Lord and Saviour Jesus Christ.

Our Father, *once.*   Hail Mary, *ten times.*

Glory be to the Father, *once.*

Let us pray.

O HOLY Mary, Queen of virgins, through the mystery of the incarnation of thy beloved Son our Lord Jesus Christ, by which our salvation was so happily begun; obtain for us, through thy intercession, light to be aware of the greatness of the benefit which he has bestowed on us, in becoming our brother, and in making thee, his Mother, our Mother also. Amen.

II. THE VISITATION

Let us contemplate in this mystery, how the Blessed Virgin Mary, understanding from the angel that her cousin St Elizabeth had conceived, went with haste into the mountains of Judea to visit her, and remained with her three months.

Our Father, *once.*   Hail Mary, *ten times.*

Glory be to the Father, *once.*

Let us pray.

O HOLY Virgin, spotless mirror of humility, by that charity which moved thee to visit thy holy cousin, obtain for us, through thy intercession, that our hearts being visited by thy holy Son and freed from all sin, we may praise and give thanks for ever. Amen.

III. THE BIRTH OF OUR SAVIOUR JESUS CHRIST IN BETHLEHEM

Let us contemplate in this mystery, how the Blessed Virgin Mary, when the time of her delivery was come, brought forth our Redeemer Jesus Christ at Bethlehem, and laid him in a manger, because there was no room for him in the inn.

Our Father, *once.*   Hail Mary, *ten times.*

Glory be to the Father, *once.*

Let us pray.

Most pure Mother of God, through thy virginal and joyful delivery, whereby thou gavest unto the world thy only Son our Saviour; we beseech thee, obtain for us, through thy intercession, the grace to lead such pure and holy lives that we may become worthy to sing without ceasing the mercies of thy Son and his benefits to us through thee. Amen.

IV. THE PRESENTATION OF OUR BLESSED LORD IN THE TEMPLE

Let us contemplate in this mystery, how the Blessed Virgin Mary, on the day of her purification, presented the child Jesus in the Temple, where holy Simeon, devoutly giving thanks to God, received him into his arms.

Our Father, *once.* Hail Mary, *ten times.*

Glory be to the Father, *once.*

Let us pray.

O HOLY Virgin, admirable pattern of obedience, who didst present in the temple the Lord of the temple; obtain for us, of thy beloved Son, that with Simeon and Anna we may praise and glorify him for ever. Amen.

V. THE FINDING OF THE CHILD JESUS IN THE TEMPLE

Let us contemplate in this mystery, how the Blessed Virgin Mary, after having lost her beloved Son in Jerusalem, and sought him for the space of three days, found him at last, on the third day, discoursing with the doctors in the temple.

Our Father, *once.* Hail Mary, *ten times.*

Glory be to the Father, *once.*

Let us pray.

BLESSED Virgin, more than martyr in thy sufferings, and the comfort of such as are afflicted; by that unspeakable joy wherewith thy soul was ravished at finding thy Son in the temple, obtain of him that we may seek him, and find him in the holy Catholic Church, and be never more separated from him. Amen.

SALVE REGINA

HAIL, holy Queen, Mother of Mercy, hail, our life, our sweetness, and our hope! To thee do we cry, poor banished children of Eve; to thee do we send up our sighs, mourning and weeping in this vale of tears. Turn, then, most gracious advocate, thy eyes of mercy towards us; and after this our exile, show unto us the blessed fruit of thy womb, Jesus. O clement, O loving, O sweet Virgin Mary.

℣ Pray for us, O holy Mother of God.

℟ That we may be made worthy of the promises of Christ.

Let us pray.

O GOD, whose only-begotten Son, by his life, death, and resurrection, has purchased for us the rewards of eternal life; grant, we beseech thee, that, meditating upon these mysteries, in the most holy Rosary of the Blessed Virgin Mary, we may both imitate what they contain, and obtain what they promise. Through the same Christ our Lord. Amen.

THE DOLOROUS OR SORROWFUL MYSTERIES

For Tuesdays and Fridays throughout the year, and the Sundays in Lent.

I. THE PRAYER AND BLOODY SWEAT OF OUR BLESSED SAVIOUR IN THE GARDEN

Let us contemplate in this mystery, how our Lord Jesus Christ was so afflicted for us in the Garden of Gethsemane, that his body was bathed in a sweat of blood, which ran down in great drops upon the ground.

Our Father, *once*.   Hail Mary, *ten times*.

Glory be to the Father, *once*.

Let us pray.

MOST holy Virgin, more than martyr, by that ardent prayer, which thy Son poured forth to his Father in the garden, intercede for us, that our passions may be reduced to the obedience of reason, and that we ourselves may always be subject to the will of God. Amen.

II. THE SCOURGING OF OUR BLESSED LORD AT THE PILLAR

Let us contemplate in this mystery, how our Lord Jesus Christ, before being delivered up by Pilate to the fury of the Jews, was cruelly scourged at a pillar.

Our Father, *once*.   Hail Mary, *ten times*.

Glory be to the Father, *once*.

Let us pray.

O MOTHER of God, overflowing fountain of patience, through those stripes which thy Son endured for us; obtain of him the grace that we may know how to mortify our rebellious senses, and avoid all occasions of sin. Amen.

III. THE CROWNING OF OUR BLESSED SAVIOUR WITH THORNS

Let us contemplate in this mystery, how cruel ministers of Satan plaited a crown of sharp thorns, and pressed it on the sacred head of our Lord Jesus Christ.

Our Father, *once*.   Hail Mary, *ten times*.

Glory be to the Father, *once*.

Let us pray.

O MOTHER of our eternal Prince and King of Glory, by those sharp thorns, wherewith his most holy head was pierced, we beseech thee that we may be delivered, through thy intercession, from all motions of pride, and, in the day of judgement, from that confusion which our sins deserve. Amen.

IV. JESUS CARRYING HIS CROSS

Let us contemplate in this mystery, how our Lord Jesus Christ, being sentenced to die, patiently bore the cross which was laid upon his shoulders for his greater torment and ignominy.

Our Father, *once*.   Hail Mary, *ten times*.

Glory be to the Father, *once*.

Let us pray.

O HOLY Virgin, example of patience, by the painful carrying of the cross, in which thy Son our Lord Jesus Christ bore the heavy weight of our sins, obtain for us, through thy intercession, courage and strength to follow his steps and to bear our cross after him, to the end of our lives. Amen.

V. THE CRUCIFIXION AND DEATH OF OUR LORD

Let us contemplate in this mystery, how our Lord Jesus Christ, being come to Mount Calvary, was stripped of his clothes, and his hands and feet were nailed to the cross, on which he died in the presence of his afflicted Mother.

Our Father, *once.*   Hail Mary, *ten times.*

Glory be to the Father, *once.*

Let us pray.

O HOLY Mary, Mother of God, as the body of thy beloved Son was extended for us on the cross, so may we desire to be daily more and more generous in his service, and may our hearts be wounded with compassion for his bitter sufferings; and thou, O Blessed Virgin, graciously help us, by thy powerful intercession, to accomplish the work of our salvation. Amen.

SALVE REGINA

HAIL, holy Queen, Mother of Mercy, hail, our life, our sweetness, and our hope! To thee do we cry, poor banished children of Eve; to thee do we send up our sighs, mourning and weeping in this vale of tears. Turn, then, most gracious advocate, thy eyes of mercy towards us; and after this our exile, show unto us the blessed fruit of thy womb, Jesus. O clement, O loving, O sweet Virgin Mary.

℣ Pray for us, O holy Mother of God.

℟ That we may be made worthy of the promises of

Christ.

Let us pray.

O GOD, whose only-begotten Son, by his life, death, and resurrection, has purchased for us the rewards of eternal life; grant, we beseech thee, that, meditating upon these mysteries, in the most holy Rosary of the Blessed Virgin Mary, we may both imitate what they contain, and obtain what they promise. Through the same Christ our Lord. Amen.

THE GLORIOUS MYSTERIES

For Wednesdays and Saturdays throughout the year, and the Sundays from Easter till Advent.

I. THE RESURRECTION

Let us contemplate in this mystery, how our Lord Jesus Christ triumphed gloriously over death, and rose again on the third day.

Our Father, *once.*   Hail Mary, *ten times.*

Glory be to the Father, *once.*

Let us pray.

O GLORIOUS Virgin Mary, by that unspeakable joy which was thine at the resurrection of thy Son, obtain of him, for us, that our hearts may never go astray after the false joys of this world, but may be ever employed in the pursuit of the true and solid joys of heaven. Amen.

II. THE ASCENSION OF CHRIST INTO HEAVEN

Let us contemplate in this mystery, how our Lord Jesus Christ, forty days after his resurrection, ascended into heaven, attended by angels, before the eyes of his holy Mother and of his holy apostles and disciples.

Our Father, *once.*   Hail Mary, *ten times.*

Glory be to the Father, *once.*

Let us pray.

O MOTHER of God, comfort of the afflicted, as thy beloved Son, when he ascended into heaven, lifted up his hands and blessed his apostles, so lift up thy pure hands to him for us, that we may enjoy his blessing and thine also, both on earth and hereafter in heaven. Amen.

III. THE DESCENT OF THE HOLY GHOST ON THE APOSTLES

Let us contemplate in this mystery, how our Lord Jesus Christ, being seated at the right hand of God, sent, as he had promised, the Holy Ghost upon his apostles, who had returned to Jerusalem, and had continued in prayer with the Blessed Virgin Mary, expecting the performance of his promise.

Our Father, *once.*   Hail Mary, *ten times.*

Glory be to the Father, *once.*

Let us pray.

O SACRED Virgin, tabernacle of the Holy Ghost, we beseech thee, obtain by thy intercession, that this Comforter, whom thy beloved Son sent down upon his apostles, may teach us the true way to salvation, and make us walk in the paths of virtue and good works. Amen.

IV. THE ASSUMPTION OF THE BLESSED VIRGIN MARY INTO HEAVEN

Let us contemplate in this mystery, how the glorious Virgin, twelve years after the resurrection of her son, passed out of this world unto him, and, accompanied by the holy angels, was assumed body and soul into heaven.

Our Father, *once.*   Hail Mary, *ten times.*

Glory be to the Father, *once.*

Let us pray.

MOST prudent Virgin, who entering the heavenly palace, didst fill the holy angels with joy, and man with hope, intercede for us at the hour of our death; that we may be delivered from the illusions and temptations of the devil, and pass joyfully out of this temporal state into the happiness of eternal life. Amen.

V. THE CORONATION OF THE BLESSED VIRGIN MARY IN HEAVEN, AND THE GLORY OF ALL THE SAINTS

Let us contemplate in this mystery, how the glorious Virgin Mary, to the great jubilee and exultation of the whole court of heaven, was crowned by her Son with the brightest diadem of glory, and how all the saints rejoice with her in bliss.

Our Father, *once*.   Hail Mary, *ten times*.

Glory be to the Father, *once*.

Let us pray.

O GLORIOUS Queen of heaven, accept this Rosary which we offer as a crown of roses at thy feet, and grant, gracious Lady, that our hearts may be inflamed with desire to see thee in thy glory, a desire so ardent that it may never die in us until it gives place to its happy fruition. Amen.

SALVE REGINA

HAIL, holy Queen, Mother of Mercy, hail, our life, our sweetness, and our hope! To thee do we cry, poor banished children of Eve; to thee do we send up our sighs, mourning and weeping in this vale of tears. Turn, then, most gracious advocate, thy eyes of mercy towards us; and after this our exile, show unto us the blessed fruit of thy womb, Jesus. O clement, O loving, O sweet Virgin Mary.

℣ Pray for us, O holy Mother of God.

℟ That we may be made worthy of the promises of Christ.

Let us pray.

O GOD, whose only-begotten Son, by his life, death, and resurrection, has purchased for us the rewards of eternal life; grant, we beseech thee, that, meditating upon these mysteries, in the most holy Rosary of the Blessed Virgin Mary, we may both imitate what they contain, and obtain what they promise. Through the same Christ our Lord. Amen.

ANCIENT WALSINGHAM PRAYER

Alone of all women, mother and virgin, mother most happy, virgin most pure, behold we, sinful as we are, come to see thee who art all pure. We salute thee, we honour thee as how we may with our humble offerings. May thy Son grant us that imitating thy most holy manners we also, by the grace of the Holy Spirit, may all deserve to conceive the child Jesus in our inmost hearts, and, once conceived, never to lose him. Amen.

PART III:

PRIVATE DEVOTIONS

PRAYERS FOR CONFESSION

Prayer Before an
Examination of Conscience

I am perfectly sensible, O my God, that I have in many ways offended thy divine majesty, and provoked thy wrath by my sins; and that if I obtain not pardon I shall be cast out of thy sight forever. I desire, therefore, at present to call myself to an account, and look into all the sins whereby I have displeased thee; but O my God, how miserably shall I deceive myself if thou assist me not in this work by thy heavenly light. Grant me, therefore, at present, thy grace, whereby I may discover all my imperfections, see all my failings, and duly call to mind all my sins: for I know that nothing is hidden from thy sight. But I confess myself in the dark as to my own failings: my passions blind me, self-love flatters me, presumption deludes me, and though I have many sins which stare me in the face, and cannot be hidden, yet how many, too, are there quite concealed from me! But discover even those to me, O Lord! Enlighten my darkness, cure my blindness, and remove every veil that hides my sins from me, that I may be no longer a secret to myself, nor a stranger to my own failings, not ever flatter myself with the thoughts of having repented, and at the same time nourish folly and vice within my breast. Come, Holy Ghost, and by a beam of thy divine light illumine my understanding, that I may have a perfect view of all my sins and iniquities, and that, sincerely repenting of them, I may know thee, and be again received into thy favour. Amen.

Initial Examination of Conscience

Begin by examining yourself on your last confession. Ask whether a grievous sin was forgotten through want of proper examination, or concealed or disguised through shame. Whether you confessed without a true sorrow and a firm purpose of amendment. Whether you have repaired evil done to your neighbour. Whether the penance was performed without voluntary distractions. Whether you have neglected your confessor's counsel and fallen at once into habitual sins.

Then examine yourself on the Ten Commandments; the Commandments of the Church; the Seven Capital sins; the duties of your state of life; and your ruling passion. Calmly recall the different occasions of sin which have fallen in your way, or to which your state and condition in life expose you; the places you have frequented; the persons with whom you have associated. Do not neglect to consider the circumstances which alter the grievousness of the sin, nor the various ways in which we become accessory to the sins of others.

The Ten Commandments

I. Thou shalt not have strange gods before me. Thou shalt not make to thyself any graven thing, nor the likeness of anything that is in the heaven above, or in the earth beneath, nor of these things that are in the waters under the earth. Thou shalt not adore them nor serve them.

II. Thou shalt not take the name of the Lord thy God in vain.

III. Remember that thou keep holy the Lord's day.

IV. Honour thy father and thy mother.

V. Thou shalt not kill.

VI. Thou shalt not commit adultery.

VII. Thou shalt not steal.

VIII. Thou shalt not bear false witness against thy neighbour.

IX. Thou shalt not covet thy neighbour's wife.

X. Thou shalt not covet thy neighbour's goods.

The Six Precepts of the Church

1. To keep the Sundays and Holy days of Obligation holy, by hearing Mass and resting from servile works.
2. To observe the appointed days of penance.
3. To go to confession at least once a year.
4. To receive the Blessed Sacrament at least once a year, and that at Easter or thereabouts.
5. To contribute to the support of our pastors.
6. Not to marry within certain degrees of kindred.

The Seven Deadly Sins
Pride—Avarice—Lust—Anger—Gluttony—Envy—Sloth

A Method of Examination of Conscience
According to the threefold Duty we owe:
(I) To God.
(II) To our Neighbour.
(III) To ourselves.

I. In Relation To God

1. Have you omitted morning or evening prayer, or neglected to make your daily examination of conscience? Have you prayed negligently, and with wilful distraction?

2. Have you spent your time, especially on Sundays and holidays, not in sluggishly lying abed, or in any sort of idle entertainment, but in reading, praying, or other pious exercises; and taken care that those under your charge have done the like, and not wanted the instructions necessary for their condition, nor time for prayer, or to prepare for the sacraments?

3. Have you spoken irreverently of God and holy things? Have you taken his name in vain, or told untruths?

4. Have you omitted your duty through human respect, interest, compliance, etc. ?

5. Have you been zealous for God's honour, for justice, virtue and truth, and reproved such as act otherwise?

6. Have you resigned your will to God in troubles, necessities, sickness, etc. ?

7. Have you faithfully resisted thoughts of infidelity, distrust, presumption, impurity, etc.?

II. In Relation To Your Neighbour

1. Have you disobeyed your superiors, murmured against their commands, or spoken of them contemptuously?

2. Have you been troubled, peevish, or impatient, when told of your faults, and not corrected them? Have you scorned the good advice of others, or censured their proceedings?

3. Have you offended any one by injurious threatening words or actions?

4. Or lessened their reputation by any sort of detractions; or in any matter of importance?

5. Or spread any report, true or false, that exposed your neighbour to contempt, or made him undervalued?

6. Have you been carrying stories backward and forward, creating discord and misunderstanding between neighbours?

7. Have you been irritable or peevish towards any one in your carriage, speech, or conversation?

8. Or taken pleasure to vex, mortify, or provoke them to swear, curse, or any ways offend God?

9. Have you mocked or reproached them for their corporal or spiritual imperfections?

10. Have you been excessive in reprehending those under your care, or been wanting in giving them just reproof?

11. Have you borne with their oversights and imperfections, and given them good counsel?

12. Have you been solicitous for such as are under your charge, and provided for their souls and bodies?

III. In Relation To Yourself.

1. Have you been obstinate in following your own will, or in defending your own opinion, in things either indifferent, dangerous or scandalous?

2. Have you taken pleasure in hearing yourself praised, or yielded to thoughts of vanity?

3. Have you indulged yourself in overmuch ease, or any ways yielded to sensuality?

4. Has your conversation been edifying and moderate; or have you been irritable, proud, or troublesome to others?

5. Have you spent overmuch time in play, or useless employments, and thereby omitted, or put off your devotions to unseasonable times?

Considerations To Excite True Contrition

Consider who he is, and how good and gracious he is to you, whom you have so often and so deeply offended by these sins. He made you—he made you for himself, to know, love, and serve him, and to be happy with him forever. He redeemed you by his blood. He has borne with you and waited for you so long. He it is who has called you and moved you to repentance. Why have you thus sinned against him? Why have you been so ungrateful? What more could he do for you? Be ashamed, and mourn, and despise yourself, because you have sinned against your Maker and your Redeemer whom you ought to love above all things!

Consider the consequences of even one mortal sin. By it you lose the grace of God. You destroy peace of conscience; you forfeit the felicity of heaven, for which you were created and redeemed; and you prepare for yourself eternal punishment. If we grieve for the loss of temporal and earthly things, how much more should we grieve for having deliberately exposed ourselves to the loss of those which are eternal and heavenly!

Consider how great is the love of God for you, if only from this, that he has so long waited for you, and spared you, when he might have so justly cast you into hell. Behold him fastened to the cross for love of you! Behold him pouring forth his precious Blood as a fountain to cleanse you from your sins. Hear him saying, "I thirst,"— "I thirst with an ardent desire for your salvation!" Behold him stretching out his arms to embrace you, and waiting until you should come to yourself and turn unto him, and throw yourself before him, and say, "Father, I have sinned against heaven and before you, and am no more worthy to be called your son." Let these considerations touch your heart with love for him who so loves you, and love will beget true contrition, most acceptable to God.

A Prayer For Obtaining Contrition

I have now here before me, O Lord, a sad prospect of the manifold offences whereby I have displeased thy divine Majesty, and which I am assured will appear in judgement against me if, by repentance and a hearty sorrow, my soul be not prepared to receive thy pardon. But this sorrow and this repentance, O Lord, must be the free gift of thy mercy, without which all my endeavours will be in vain, and I shall be forever miserable. Have pity, therefore, on me, O merciful Father, and pour forth into my heart thy grace, whereby I may sincerely repent of all my sins; grant me true contrition, that I may bewail my base ingratitude, and grieve from my heart for having offended so good a God. Permit me not to be deluded by a false sorrow, as I fear I have been too often, through my own weakness and neglect; but let it now be thy gift, descending from thee, the Father of Lights, that so my repentance may be accompanied by an amendment and a change of life, that being thus acquitted from the guilt of my sins, I may once more be received into the number of thy servants. Amen.

Nine Ways of Being An Accessory to Another's Sin

By counsel — By command — By consent
By provocation—By praise or flattery — By concealment
By partaking—By silence — By defending the ill done

The Sins Against the Holy Ghost

Presumption of God's mercy — Despair
Impugning the known truth
Envy at another's spiritual good
Obstinacy in sin — Final impenitence

Sins Crying to Heaven for Vengeance

Wilful murder — The sin of Sodom
Oppression of the poor
Defrauding labourers of their wages

Four Last Things to be Remembered

Death — Judgement — Hell — Heaven

A FORM OF CONFESSION

The penitent kneels down (if practical), crosses himself, and asks a blessing. This may be in the following words:
Bless me, father, for I have sinned.
The priest gives a blessing.
It is … since my last confession. I confess to Almighty God, and to you, father, that I have…
He may conclude by saying:
For these and for all my sins I beg pardon of God and penance and absolution of you, father.
He will be asked to make an act of contrition.

A Short Act Of Contrition:
O my God, because thou art so good, I am very sorry that I have sinned against thee, and with the help of thy grace I will not sin again.

The penitent should cross himself while the priest gives him absolution. Afterwards he should make his thanksgiving.

Thanksgiving After Confession

O most merciful God, I thank thee for thy unfailing kindness in having again received me and for all the graces and blessings thou hast bestowed upon me. In the Sacrament of Penance, my soul has been cleansed from sin in the Precious Blood of Jesus. Grant that I may abhor sin as the greatest evil and may avoid the occasions of sin; this I resolve to do with the assistance of thy grace. Bless my resolutions that they may not be in vain as so many others have been. Enable me to remain in the state of sanctifying grace, that I may save my soul.

Hail Mary, etc..

Eternal Father, I offer thee the Most Precious Blood of Jesus Christ in atonement for my sins, in supplication for the holy souls in Purgatory, and for the needs of the Holy Church. Amen.
Praised be Jesus and Mary, now and forever. Amen.

Prayers for Communion

Prayers of St. Thomas Aquinas:
before Communion

Almighty and eternal God, behold, I approach the Sacrament of thine only-begotten Son, our Lord Jesus Christ. I approach as one who is sick to the physician of life, as one unclean to the fountain of mercy, as one blind to the light of eternal brightness, as one poor and needy to the Lord of heaven and earth. Therefore I beseech thee, of thine infinite goodness, to heal my sickness, to wash away my filth, to enlighten my blindness, to enrich my poverty, and to clothe my nakedness, that I may receive the Bread of angels, the King of kings, and the Lord of lords with such reverence and humility, with such contrition and devotion, with such purity and faith, with such purpose and intention, as may conduce to the salvation of my soul. Grant, I beseech thee, that I may receive not only the Sacrament of the Body and Blood of our Lord, but also the fruit and virtue of this Sacrament. O most indulgent God, grant me so to receive the Body of thine only-begotten Son, our Lord Jesus Christ, which he took of the Virgin Mary, that I may be found worthy to be incorporated with his mystical body and numbered among his members. O most loving Father, grant that I may one day contemplate for ever, face to face. thy beloved Son, whom now on my pilgrimage I am about to receive under the sacramental veils; who liveth and reigneth with thee God, world without end. Amen.

After Communion

I give thee thanks, Lord, holy Father, almighty and eternal God, who hast been pleased, not for any merits of mine, but only out of the condescension of thy mercy, to satisfy me a sinner, thy unworthy servant, with the precious Body and Blood of thy Son our Lord Jesus Christ. And I pray that this holy communion be not to me a condemnation to punishment, but a saving plea to forgiveness. May it be to me the armour of faith and the shield of a good will. May it be the emptying out of my vices, the extinction of all concupiscence and lust, the increase of charity and patience, of humility and obedience, and of all virtues; a strong defence against the snares of all enemies, visible and invisible; the quieting of all my evil impulses, both carnal and spiritual; a firm cleaving to thee, the one true God; and the happy accomplishment of my destiny. And I pray thee, that thou wouldst be pleased to bring me, a sinner, to that banquet, wonderful past all telling, where thou, with thy Son and the Holy Ghost, art to thy Saints true light, total fulfilment, eternal joy, unalloyed gladness and perfect happiness. Through the same Christ our Lord. Amen.

Obsecro te

I beseech thee, most sweet Lord Jesus Christ, grant that thy Passion may be to me a power by which I may be strengthened, protected and defended. May thy wounds be to me food and drink, by which I may be nourished, inebriated and overjoyed. May the sprinkling of thy Blood be to me an ablution for all my sins. May thy death prove to me life everlasting, and thy cross be to me an eternal glory. In these be my refreshment, my joy, my preservation and sweetness of heart. Who livest and reignest world without end. Amen.

 ## Anima Christi

Anima Christi, sanctífica me.
Corpus Christi, salva me.
Sanguis Christi, inébria me.
Aqua láteris Christi, lava me.
Pássio Christi, confórta me.
O bone Iesu, exáudi me.
Intra tua vúlnera abscónde me.
Ne permíttas me separári a te.
Ab hoste malígno defénde me.
In hora mortis meæ voca me.
Et iube me veníre ad te,
Ut cum Sanctis tuis laudem te
In sǽcula sæculórum. Amen.

Soul of Christ, be my sanctification,
Body of Christ, be my salvation,
Blood of Christ, fill all my veins,
Water from the side of Christ, wash out my stains.
May Christ's Passion strengthen me,
O good Jesu, hear me.
In thy wounds I fain would hide,
Never to be parted from thy side.
Guard me when my foes assail me,
Call me when my life shall fail me.
That I for all eternity
With thy saints may praise thee. Amen.

Prayer before a Crucifix

Behold, O kind and most sweet Jesus, I cast myself upon my knees in thy sight, and with the most fervent desire of my soul, I pray and beseech thee that thou wouldst impress upon my heart lively sentiments of faith, hope and charity, with true contrition for my sins and a firm purpose of amendment; while with deep affection and grief of soul I ponder within myself and mentally contemplate thy five wounds, having before my eyes the words which David the prophet put on thy lips concerning thee: 'They have pierced my hands and my feet, they have numbered all my bones'.
(Ps. 21:17-18).

For the intentions of the Latin Mass Society

The Society asks that wherever possible, at 6pm each Thursday, members offer vocally or mentally, three times this short act of adoration:

O Sacrament most holy, O Sacrament Divine,
All praise and all thanksgiving be every moment thine.

O Sacraméntum sanctíssimum, O Sacraméntum divínum,
Omnis laus et grátiæ sint tibi in perpétuum.

Prayer for Persecuted Christians
Collect *Pro Ecclesiae libertate,* from the Roman Missal

Graciously hear the prayers of thy Church, we beseech thee, O Lord: that her enemies and all heresies be brought to nought, and that she may serve thee in perfect security and freedom. Through Christ our Lord. Amen.

Ecclésiae tuae, quǽsumus, Dómine, preces placátus ad-
mítte: ut, destrúctis adversitátibus et erróribus univérsis,
secúra tibi sérviat libertáte. Per Christum Dóminium
nostrum. Amen.

For the Sovereign Pontiff
From the *Manual of Prayers* (1953)

℣. Let us pray for our holy Father the Pope.

℞. The Lord preserve him, and give him life, and make him blessed upon earth, and deliver him not up to the will of his enemies.

Let us pray.

O Almighty and eternal God, have mercy on thy servant Francis, our Pope, and direct him according to thy clemency into the way of everlasting salvation; that he may desire by thy grace those things which are pleasing to thee, and perform them with all his strength. Through Christ our Lord.

℞. Amen.

The Prayer of the Sodality of St Augustine

Collect *Pro devotis amicis,* from the Roman Missal

O God, who, by the grace of the Holy Ghost, hast poured the gifts of charity in the hearts of thy faithful, grant to thy servants and handmaids, for whom we entreat thy mercy, health of mind and body; that they may love thee with all their strength and, by perfect love, may do what is pleasing to thee. Through our Lord Jesus Christ thy Son, who liveth and reigneth in the unity of the same Holy Ghost, God, world without end. Amen.

Deus, qui caritátis dona per grátiam Sancti Spíritus tuórum fidélium córdibus infudísti : da fámulis et famulábus tuis, pro quibus tuam deprecámur cleméntiam, salútem mentis et córporis ; ut te tota virtúte díligant, et quæ tibi plácita sunt, tota dilectióne perfíciant. Per Dóminum nostrum Iesum Christum Fílium tuum, qui tecum vivit et regnat in unitáte eiúsdem Spíritus Sancti, Deus, per ómnia sǽcula sæculórum. Amen.

About the Sodality of St Augustine

Members undertake to say every day the above prayer for the Sodality's intention; members who are priests undertake to say one Mass a month for this intention. The intention is the conversion or return to the Faith of family and friends of Sodality members. The Latin Mass Society, to which the Sodality is affiliated, arranges and announces in advance at least one public, Traditional Sung (or Solemn) Mass for this intention each year.

Members may add other Masses, prayers, and devotions, for the Sodality's intention, and are encouraged to do so.

Membership of the Sodality is free and open to all: simply email the Society to be added to the list of members.

PLENARY INDULGENCES

An indulgence is the remission, in whole or in part, of the temporal punishment that a penitent, whose sins are forgiven, has yet to suffer, either in this life or in purgatory. This is granted by the Church through the Power of the Keys, from the inexhaustible treasury of the merits of Christ and his saints. A Partial Indulgence remits some of the temporal punishment due: a Plenary Indulgence remits all the temporal punishment.

Indulgences can also be offered for the holy souls in purgatory, rather than for ourselves. However, indulgences offered for the holy souls are efficacious by way of suffrage, that is, depending on God's decision, since the Church on earth does not have jurisdiction over the souls in purgatory.

Four ways to gain a Plenary Indulgence
A Catholic, being in the state of grace, can gain a Plenary Indulgence by many different prayers and works of piety, but the following are four common ways of gaining an indulgence:

1. Making a visit to the Blessed Sacrament to adore Our Lord in the tabernacle for at least half an hour;
2. Spending at least half an hour reading Sacred Scripture, as spiritual reading, with the veneration due to the Word of God;
3. Making the Stations of the Cross. This includes walking from Station to Station. If publicly held, then the leader of the Stations must move from Station to Station. No specific prayers are required, but devout meditation on the passion and death of Our Lord is required;
4. Recitation of the Rosary, at least five decades, with devout meditation on the Mysteries, in addition to the vocal recitation. The Rosary must be said in a church; family group; religious community or pious association.

Additional Requirements

In addition to performing the specified works the following conditions are required:

1. Confession;
2. Holy Communion; and
3. Prayers for the Pope's intentions (one *Pater noster* and one *Ave Maria).*

These three conditions may be fulfilled within the octave before or after the completion of the prescribed work.

In addition, a person's mind and heart must be free from all attachment to sin and be truly sorry for all his venial sins. If one tries to gain a plenary indulgence, but fails to fulfil all the requirements, the indulgence will only be partial.

Only one plenary indulgence can be gained per day, except at "the moment of death" when a person may gain a second plenary indulgence for that day.

If we generously offer indulgences for the holy souls in purgatory, we may hope to obtain relief or release for many of them, in accord with God's Holy Will. In gratitude they may well obtain for us many great favours.

According to the *Enchiridion of Indulgences* (1991 edition) a plenary indulgence is granted to the Christian faithful who spend at least three full days of spiritual exercises during a retreat or mission. As the Walsingham Pilgrimage is of three days' duration and is similar to a retreat, by participating well and praying fervently during the pilgrimage one would gain a plenary indulgence, provided the usual conditions are fulfilled.

PART IV:

PILGRIMS' SONGS

CHANT: LITANIES

THE GREAT LITANY
Litany of the Saints

Ký-ri- e e-lé- i-son. ii. Christe e-lé- i-son. ii. Ký-ri- e e-lé-

i-son. ii. Christe, audi nos. ii. Christe, exáudi nos. ii.

Pa- ter de cæ- lis **De**-us, * mi-se-rére nobis.
Fili Redémptor mun-di **De**-us, * mi-se-rére nobis.
Spí- ri- tus Sancte **De**-us, * mi-se-rére nobis.
Sancta Trínitas, u- nus **De**-us, * mi-se-rére nobis.

Sancta Ma-**rí**- a, * ora pro nobis.

Sancta De- i **Génetrix**, * ora pro nobis.
Sancta Virgo **vírginum**, * ora pro nobis.
Sancte **Míchæl**, * ora pro nobis.
Sancte **Gábriel**, * ora pro nobis.
Sancte **Ráphæl**, * ora pro nobis.

Omnes sancti Angeli et Archánge-li, * orá-te pro nobis.
Omnes sancti beatórum Spirítuum **ór**-dines, * orá-te pro nobis.

Sancte Io- ánnes Bapt**ísta**, * ora pro nobis.
Sancte **Io**-seph, * ora pro nobis.

Omnes sancti Patri- árchæ et Proph**étæ**, * orá-te pro nobis.

Sancte **Petre**, * ora pro nobis.

Sáncte **Páu**le,	ora.
Sáncte And**ré**a,	ora.
Sáncte Ia**có**be,	ora.
Sáncte Io**án**nes,	ora.
Sáncte **Thó**ma,	ora.
Sáncte Ia**có**be,	ora.
Sáncte Phi**lí**ppe,	ora.
Sáncte Bartolo**mǽ**e,	ora.
Sáncte Mat**thǽ**e,	ora.
Sáncte **Sí**mon,	ora.
Sáncte Thad**dǽ**e,	ora.
Sáncte Mat**thí**a,	ora.
Sáncte **Bár**naba,	ora.
Sáncte **Lú**ca,	ora.
Sáncte **Már**ce,	ora.
Omnes sáncti Apóstoli et Evange**lí**stæ,	oráte.
Omnes sáncti Discípuli **Dó**mini,	oráte.
Omnes sáncti Inno**cén**tes,	oráte.
Sáncte **Sté**phane,	ora.
Sáncte Lau**rén**ti,	ora.
Sáncte Vin**cén**ti,	ora.
Sáncti Fabiáne et Sebastiáne,	oráte.
Sáncti Ioánnes et **Páu**le,	oráte.
Sáncti Cósma et Damiáne,	oráte.
Sáncti Gervási et Protási,	oráte.
Omnes sáncti **Már**tyres,	oráte.
Sáncte Sil**vés**ter,	ora.
Sáncte Gre**gó**ri,	ora.
Sáncte Am**bró**si,	ora.
Sáncte Augus**tí**ne,	ora.
Sáncte Hie**ró**nyme,	ora.
Sáncte Mar**tí**ne,	ora.
Sáncte Nico**lǽ**,	ora.
Omnes sáncti Pontífices et Confes**só**res,	oráte.
Omnes sancti Doc**tó**res,	oráte.
Sáncte An**tó**ni,	ora.
Sáncte Bene**dí**cte,	ora.
Sáncte Ber**nár**de,	ora.
Sáncte Do**mí**nice,	ora.

Sáncte Francísce,	or*a*.
Omnes sáncti Sacerdótes et Levítæ,	orá*te*.
Omnes sáncti Mónachi et Eremítæ,	orá*te*.
Sáncta María Magdaléna,	or*a*.
Sáncta **A**gatha,	or*a*.
Sáncta **L**úcia,	or*a*.
Sáncta **A**gnes,	or*a*.
Sáncta Cæcília,	or*a*.
Sáncta Catharína,	or*a*.
Sáncta Anast**á**sia,	or*a*.
Omnes sánctæ Vírgines et **V**íduæ,	orá*te*.
Omnes Sáncti et Sánctæ **D**éi,	intercéd*ite pro* nobis.

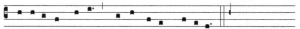

Pro-pí-*ti- us* e**s**to, * parce no-bis, Dómine.
Pro-pí-*ti- us* e**s**to, * exáu-di nos, Dómine.
  Ab *omni* **ma**-lo, * líbe- ra nos, Dómine.

Ab ómni pec**cá**to,	líbera nos, Dómine.
Ab *ira* **tu**a,	líbera nos, Dómine.
A subitánea et improv*ísa* **mór**te,	líbera nos, Dómine.
Ab insídi*is di***áb**oli,	líbera nos, Dómine.
Ab ira et ódio et omni mala *volun*tá**te**,	líbera nos, Dómine.
A spíritu forni*cati*ónis,	líbera nos, Dómine.
A fúlgure et *tempes***tá**te,	líbera nos, Dómine.
A flagéllo *terræ***mó**tus,	líbera nos, Dómine.
A peste, fa*me, et* **b**éllo,	líbera nos, Dómine.
A mórte *per***pé**tua,	líbera nos, Dómine.
Per mystérium sánctæ Incarnati*ónis* **tu**æ,	
	líbera nos, Dómine.
Per Ad*vén***tum tú**um,	líbera nos, Dómine.
Per Nativi*tátem* **tú**am,	líbera nos, Dómine.
Per Baptísmum et sánctum ieiú*nium* **tú**um,	
	líbera nos, Dómine.
Per Crucem et Passi*ónem* **tú**am,	líbera nos, Dómine.
Per Mortem et Sepul*túram* **tú**am,	líbera nos, Dómine.
Per sánctam Resurrecti*ónem* **tú**am,	líbera nos, Dómine.
Per admirábilem Ascensi*ónem* **tú**am,	líbera nos, Dómine.
Per ad*vén*tum Spíritus Sán*cti Pa***rá**cliti,	líbera nos, Dómine.

Pecca- **tó**res, ✱ te rogámus, audi nos.

In dí*e iu***dí**cii,   líbera nos, Dómine.
Ut nó*bis* **pár**cas,   te rogámus, áudi nos.
Ut nóbis *in***dúl**geas,   te rogámus, áudi nos.
Ut ad véram pænituéntiam nos perdúcere *dig***né**ris,
                                         te rogámus, áudi nos.
Ut Ecclésiam túam sánctam † régere et conserváre
    *dig***né**ris,   te rogámus, áudi nos.
Ut Dómnum Apostólicum et omnes ecclesiásticos órdines
    † in sáncta religióne conserváre *dig***né**ris,
                                         te rogámus, áudi nos.
Ut inimícos sánctæ Ecclésiæ † humiliáre *dig***né**ris,
                                         te rogámus, áudi nos.
Ut régibus et princípibus christiánis † pácem et véram
    concórdiam donáre *dig***né**ris, te rogámus, áudi nos.
Ut cuncto pópulo christiáno † pácem et unitátem largíri
    *dig***né**ris,   te rogámus, áudi nos.
Ut omnes errántes ad unitátem Ecclésiæ revocáre, † et
    infidéles univérsos ad Evangélii lúmen perdúcere
    *dig***né**ris,   te rogámus, áudi nos.
Ut nosmetípsos in tuo sancto servítio † confortáre et con
    serváre *dig***né**ris,   te rogámus, áudi nos.
Ut mentes nostras † ad cæléstia desidéria érigas,
                                         te rogámus, áudi nos.
Ut ómnibus benefactóribus nostris † sempitérna bóna
    *re***trí**buas,   te rogámus, áudi nos.
Ut ánimas nostras, † fratrum, propinquórum et bene-
    factórum nostrórum † ab ætérna damnatióne *e***rí**pias,
                                         te rogámus, áudi nos.
Ut frúctus térræ † dáre et conserváre *dig***né**ris,
                                         te rogámus, áudi nos.
Ut ómnibus fidélibus defúnctis † réquiem ætérnam
    donáre *dig***né**ris,   te rogámus, áudi nos.
Ut nos exaudíre *dig***né**ris,   te rogámus, áudi nos.
Fi*li* **Dé**i,   te rogámus, áudi nos.

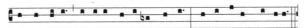

Agnus De-i, qui tollis peccá-ta mundi, * parce nobis, Dómine.

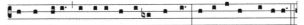

Agnus De-i, qui tollis peccá-ta mundi, * exáudi nos, Dómine.

Agnus De-i, qui tollis peccáta mundi, * mi-seré-re no-bis.

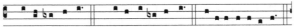

Christe, audi nos. Christe, exáudi nos Kýri- e e-lé- i-son.

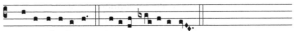

Christe e-lé- i-son. Kýri- e e-lé- i-son.

LITANY OF LORETO
in honour of the Blessed Virgin Mary

Kyri- e e-lé- i-son. *ij.* Christe e-lé- i-son. *ij.* Kýri- e e-lé-i-son. *ij.* Christe, audi nos. *ij.* Christe, exáudi nos. *ij.*

Pa- ter de *cœ-* lis **De**-us, * mi-se-ré-re nobis.
Fili Redémptor *mun-*di **De**-us, * mi-se-ré-re nobis.
Spí- ri- tus *Sancte* **De**-us, * mi-se-ré-re nobis.
Sancta Trínitas, *u-* nus **De**-us, * mi-se-ré-re nobis.

Sancta **Ma-** rí- a, * ora pro nobis.

Sáncta *Déi* **Gén**etrix,
Sáncta *Vírgo* **vír**ginum,
Máter **Chrí**sti,
Máter Ecclésiæ,
Máter Div*ínæ* **grá**tiæ,

Máter *purís*sima,
Máter *castís*sima,
Máter in*viol*á**ta**,
Máter in*teme*r**á**ta,
Máter *a***má**bilis,

140

Máter *admi*rábilis,
Máter bó*ni con*síli,
Máter *Crea*tóris,
Máter *Salva*tóris,
Vírgo *prudentís*sima,
Vírgo *vene*ránda,
Vírgo *prædi*cánda,
Vírgo potens,
Vírgo clemens,
Vírgo *fi*délis,
Spéc*ulum ius*títiæ,
Sédes *sapi*éntiæ,
Cáusa nos*træ læ*títiæ,
Vas spiritu*á*le,
Vas *hono*rábile,
Vas insígne de*voti*ónis,
Rósa mýstica,
Túr*ris Da*vídica,
Túr*ris e*búrnea,
Domus áurea,
Foéd*eris* árca,

Iá*nua* cǽli,
Stélla *matu*tína,
Sálus *infir*mórum,
Refúgium *pecca*tórum,
Consolátrix *afflic*tórum,
Auxílium Christi*a*nórum,
Regína *Ange*lórum,
Regína Patri*ar*chárum,
Regína *Prophe*tárum,
Regína A*posto*lórum,
Regína Mártyrum,
Regína *Confes*sórum,
Regína Vírginum,
Regína Sanc*tórum* ómnium,
Regína sine lábe origin*á*li
    *con*cépta,
Regína in cǽ*lum as*súmpta,
Regína Sacratíssi*mi Ro*sárii,
Regína fa*mili*árum,
Regína pácis,

Agnus De-i, qui tollis peccáta mundi, * parce nobis Dómine.

Agnus De-i, qui tollis peccáta mundi, * exáudi nos Dómine.

Agnus De-i, qui tollis peccáta mundi, * mi-seré-re no-bis.

℣. Ora pro nobis, Sancta Dei Génetrix.

℟. Ut digni efficiámur promissiónibus Christi.

Orémus. Concéde nos fámulos tuos, quǽsumus, Dómine Deus, perpétua mentis et córporis sanitáte gaudére: † et gloriósa beátæ Maríæ semper Vírginis intercessióne, * a præsénti liberári tristítia, et ætérna pérfrui lætítia. Per Christum Dóminum nostrum.

℟. Amen.

LITANY OF THE SACRED HEART

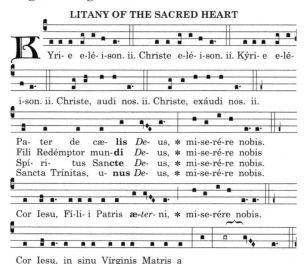

Kýri- e e-lé- i-son. ii. Christe e-lé- i-son. ii. Kýri- e e-lé-

i-son. ii. Christe, audi nos. ii. Christe, exáudi nos. ii.

Pa- ter de cæ- **lis** *De*- us, * mi-se-ré-re nobis.
Fili Redémptor mun-**di** *De*- us, * mi-se-ré-re nobis
Spí- ri- tus Sancte *De*- us, * mi-se-ré-re nobis.
Sancta Trínitas, u- **nus** *De*- us, * mi-se-ré-re nobis.

Cor Iesu, Fí-li- i Patris **æ**-*ter*- ni, * mi-se-rére nobis.

Cor Iesu, in sinu Vírginis Matris a
Spíritu Sancto **for**- *má*- tum,

Cor Iésu, Vérbo Déi substantiáliter u*ní*tum,
Cor Iésu, majestátis in*fi*nítæ,
Cor Iésu, témplum Déi *sá*nctum,
Cor Iésu, tabernáculum **Altíss**imi,
Cor Iésu, dómus Déi et pór**ta** *cǽ*li,
Cor Iésu, fórnax árdens cari*tá*tis,
Cor Iésu, justítiæ et amóris re**ceptá**cu*lum,
Cor Iésu, bonitáte et amóre *plé*num,
Cor Iésu, virtútum ómnium a*bý*ssus,
Cor Iésu, ómni láude **digníss**imum,
Cor Iésu, rex et céntrum ómni**um cór**di*um,
Cor Iésu, in quo sunt ómnes thesáuri sapiéntiæ et
sciéntiæ,
Cor Iésu, in quo hábitat ómnis plenitúdo divi**ni**tá*tis,
Cor Iésu, in quo Páter síbi bene **complá**cu*it,
Cor Iésu, de cúius plenitúdine ómnes nos **accé**pimus,
Cor Iésu, desidérium cóllium æter*nó*rum,
Cor Iésu, pátiens et múltæ mise**ricór**diæ,
Cor Iésu, díves in ómnes qui ín**vo**cant te,
Cor Iésu, fons vítæ et san**cti**tá*tis,

Cor Iésu, propitiátio pro peccátis *nó*stris,

Cor Iésu, saturátum **oppró***bri*is,

Cor Iésu, attrítum própter scéle**ra** *nó*stra,

Cor Iésu, usque ad mórtem obédi**ens** *fá*ctum,

Cor Iésu, láncea per**for***á*tum,

Cor Iésu, fons totíus consola**ti***ó*nis,

Cor Iésu, víta et resurréctio *nó*stra,

Cor Iésu, pax et reconciliátio *nó*stra,

Cor Iésu, víctima pec**ca***tó*rum,

Cor Iésu, sálus in te **sperán***ti*um,

Cor Iésu, spes in te mo**rién***ti*um,

Cor Iésu, delíciæ sanctó**rum** **ó***mni*um.

Agnus De- i, qui tollis peccáta mundi, ∗ parce nobis, Dómine.

Agnus De- i, qui tollis peccáta mundi, ∗ exáu-di nos, Dómine.

Agnus De- i, qui tollis peccáta mundi, ∗ mi-se- ré-re no-bis.

℣. Iésu, mitis et húmilis Córde,

℟. Fac cor nóstrum secúndum Cor tuum.

Orémus.

Omnípotens sempitérne Deus, réspice in Cor dilectíssimi Fílii tui et in laudes et satisfactiónes, quas in nómine peccatórum tibi persólvit, † iísque misericórdiam tuam peténtibus, Tu véniam concéde placátus ∗ in nómine ejúsdem Fílii tui Iésu Christi, qui tecum vivit et regnat in unitáte Spríritus Sancti Deus, per ómnia sǽcula sæculórum.

℟ . Amen.

LITANY OF ST JOSEPH

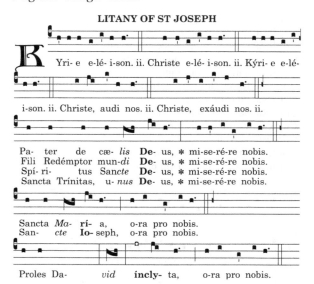

Kyri- e e-lé- i-son. ii. Christe e-lé- i-son. ii. Kýri- e e-lé-

i-son. ii. Christe, audi nos. ii. Christe, exáudi nos. ii.

Pa- ter de cæ- *lis* **De**- us, * mi-se-ré-re nobis.
Fili Redémptor mun-*di* **De**- us, * mi-se-ré-re nobis.
Spí- ri- tus San*cte* **De**- us, * mi-se-ré-re nobis.
Sancta Trínitas, u- *nus* **De**- us, * mi-se-ré-re nobis.

Sancta *Ma-* **rí-** a, o-ra pro nobis.
San- *cte* **Io-** seph, o-ra pro nobis.

Proles Da- *vid* **incly-** ta, o-ra pro nobis.

Lumen Patri*archá*rum,
Dei Genet*rícis* **Spon**se,
Custos pudi*ce* **Vírgi**nis,
Fílii Dei *nutríc*ie,
Christi defén*sor* **sédu**le,
Almæ Famíliæ **præ**ses,
Iósef *iustíssi*me,
Iósef *castíssi*me,
Iósef pru*dentíssi*me,
Iósef *fortíssi*me,
Iósef oboedi*entíssi*me,
Iósef fi*delíssi*me,

Spéculum pa*tiénti*æ,
Amátor pau*pertá*tis,
Exémplar *opífi*cum,
Domésticæ vi*tæ* **de**cus,
Cu*stos* **vírg**inum,
Familiá*rum* **cólu**men,
Solátium mi*serór*um,
Spes ægro*tánti*um,
Patróne mo*riénti*um,
Ter*ror* **dæ**monum,
Protéctor sanctæ
    *Ec***clési**æ,

Agnus De-i, qui tollis peccáta mundi, parce nobis, Dómi-ne.

Agnus De-i, qui tollis peccáta mundi, exáudi nos, Dómi-ne.

Agnus De-i, qui tollis peccáta mundi, mise-ré-re no- bis.

℣. Constítuit eum dóminum domus suæ.

℟. Et príncipem omnis possessiónis suæ.

Orémus

Deus, qui in ineffábili providéntia beátum Ióseph sanc-
tíssimæ Genetrícis tuæ Sponsum elígere dignátus es, †
præsta, quǽsumus, ut quem protectórem venerámur in
terris, * intercessórem habére mereámur in cælis: Qui
vivis et regnas in sǽcula sæculórum.

℟. Amen.

ANTIPHON : SUB TUUM PRAESIDIUM

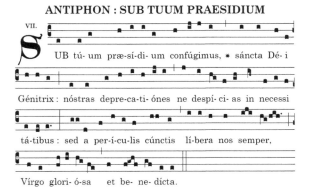

SUB tú- um præ-sí-di- um confúgimus, * sáncta Dé- i

Génitrix : nóstras depre-ca-ti- ónes ne despí- ci- as in necessi

tá-tibus : sed a per-í-cu-lis cúnctis lí-bera nos semper,

Vírgo glori- ó-sa et be- ne- dícta.

LATIN HYMNS, SEQUENCES ETC.

CRUX FIDELIS

Crux fi-dé-lis, inter omnes Arbor una nóbi- lis : nul-

la talem silva pro-fert Flore, fronde, gérmi- ne ; Dulce lig-

num, dulce clavos, dulce pondus sústi- nens.

Pange, lingua, glo-ri- ó- si Prœ-li- um cer-támi-nis Et

su-per cru- cis trophǽ- o Dic tri- úmphum nóbi- lem : Quá-

li- ter Red-émptor orbis Immo-lá- tus ví-ce- rit. Crux.

2. De pa-réntis pro-toplásti Fraude factor cóndo-lens, Quan-

do pomi noxi- á-lis Morte morsu córru- it, Ipse li-

gnum tunc no- távit, Damna ligni ut sólve- ret. Dulce.

3. Hoc opus nostræ salú- tis Ordo depo- pósce- rat : Multi-

fórmis perdi- tó-ris Arte ut artem fálle- ret, Et me-dé

lam ferret inde Hostis unde læse- rat. Crux.

4. Quando venit ergo sacri Pleni-túdo tempo- ris, Missus

est ab arce Patris Natus, orbis Cóndi- tor : Atque ventre

virgi- ná- li Carne factus pródi- it. Dulce.

5. Vagit infans inter arcta Cóndi-tus præ-sépi- a: Membra

pannis invo- lú-ta Virgo mater álli- gat, Et pe- des ma-

núsque, cru-ra, Stricta pingit fásci- a. Crux.

6. Lustra sex qui iam perá-cta, Tempus implens córpo- ris,

Se vo- lénte, natus ad hoc, Passi- ó- ni dédi- tus, Agnus

in cru- cis le- vátur Immo-lándus stí-pi- te. Dulce

7. Hic a-cétum, fel, arúndo, Spu-ta, clavi, lánce- a: Mi-te

corpus perfo- rá-tur; Sanguis, unda próflu- it, Terra, pon-

tus, astra, mundus, Quo lavántur flúmi- ne.   Crux

8. Flecte ramos, arbor al-ta, Tensa laxa vísce-ra, Et ri- gor

lentéscat ille   Quem dedit na- tívi- tas, Ut su- pérni mem-

bra re-gis Mi- te tendas stí-pi- te.   Dulce

9. Hoc opus nostræ salú- tis   Ordo depo- pósce- rat: Multi-

fórmis perdi- tó-ris   Arte ut artem fálle- ret, Et me- dé

lam ferret inde   Hostis unde lǽse- rat.   Crux.

10. So-la digna tu fu-í-sti   Ferre pré-*ti*-um sǽcu- li, Atque

portum præpa- rá-re   Nauta mundo náufra- go, Quem sa-

cer cru- or per- únxit, Fusus Agni córpo- re.   Dulce

11. Gló-ri- a et honor De- o Usquequo Al-tíssi-mo, Una

Patri Fi-li- óque, Incli- to Pa-rácli- to, Cu-i laus est et

pot- éstas Per æ-térna sǽcu- la. Amen. Crux.

SEQUENCE : INVIOLATA

Nvi- o-lá-ta, * íntegra, et casta es Marí- a: Quæ es ef-

fécta fúlgida cæli porta. O Mater alma Christi ca-ríssima:

Súscipe pi-a laudum præcóni- a. Te nunc flá-gi-tant devó-ta

corda et or-a: Nostra ut pura péctora sint et córpora. Tu-a

per precáta dulcí-sona, Nobis concédas véni- am per sǽ-cula.

O benígna! O Regí-na! O Marí- a, Quæ so-la invi-o-lá-

ta perman-sí- sti.

149

STABAT MATER

Tabat Ma-ter do-lo- rósa   Iuxta crucem lacrimósa,

Dum pendébat Fí- li- us.

Cuius animam gementem,
contristatam et dolentem
pertransivit gladius.

O quam tristis et afflicta
fuit illa benedicta,
mater Unigeniti!

Quæ mærebat et dolebat,
pia Mater, dum videbat
nati poenas inclyti.

Quis est homo qui non fleret,
matrem Christi si videret
in tanto supplicio?

Quis non posset contristari
Christi Matrem contemplari
dolentem cum Filio?

Pro peccatis suæ gentis
vidit Iesum in tormentis,
et flagellis subditum.

Vidit suum dulcem Natum
moriendo desolatum,
dum emisit spiritum.

Eia, Mater, fons amoris
me sentire vim doloris
fac, ut tecum lugeam.

Fac, ut ardeat cor meum
in amando Christum Deum
ut sibi complaceam.

Sancta Mater, istud agas,
crucifixi fige plagas

cordi meo valide.

Tui Nati vulnerati,
tam dignati pro me pati,
poenas mecum divide.

Fac me tecum pie flere,
crucifixo condolere,
donec ego vixero.

Juxta Crucem tecum stare,
et me tibi sociare
in planctu desidero.

Virgo virginum præclara,
mihi iam non sis amara,
fac me tecum plangere.

Fac, ut portem Christi
            mortem,
passionis fac consortem,
et plagas recolere.

Fac me plagis vulnerari,
fac me Cruce inebriari,
et cruore Filii.

Flammis ne urar succensus,
per te, Virgo, sim defensus
in die iudicii.

Christe, cum sit hinc exire,
da per Matrem me venire
ad palmam victoriæ.

Quando corpus morietur,
fac, ut animæ donetur
paradisi gloria. Amen.

O FILII ET FILIÆ

Lle-lú-ia, alle- lú- ia, alle-lú-ia. *Repeat* Allelúia.

1. O fí-li- i et fí-li- æ, Rex cælestis, Rex gló- ri- æ, Morte

surré- xit hó-di- e, alle-lú-ia. ℟. Allelúia.

Ex mane prima Sábbati
ad óstium monuménti
accessérunt discípuli.
Allelúia.

Et María Magdaléne,
et Iacóbi, et Salóme
Venérunt corpus úngere
Allelúia.

In albis sedens angelus
prædíxit muliéribus:
In Galilǽa est Dóminus.
Allelúia.

Et Ioánnes apóstolus
cucúrrit Petro cítius,
monuménto venit prius.
Allelúia.

Discípulis adstántibus,
in médio stetit Christus,
dicens: Pax vobis ómnibus.
Allelúia.

Ut intelléxit Didymus
quía surréxerat Iesus,
remánsit fere dúbius.
Allelúia.

Vide Thoma, vide latus,
vide pedes, vide manus,
noli esse incrédulus.
Allelúia.

Quando Thomas vidit
        Christum,
pedes, manus, latus suum,
dixit: Tu es Deus meus.
Allelúia.

Beáti qui non vidérunt
et fírmiter credidérunt;
vitam ætérnam habébunt.
Allelúia.

In hoc fésto sanctissimo
sit laus et iubilátio:
BENEDICAMUS DOMINO.
Allelúia.

Ex quíbus nos humíllimas
devótas atque débitas
DEO dicamus GRATIAS.
Allelúia.

ATTENDE DOMINE

Tténde Dómine, et mi-serére, qui-a peccávimus ti-bi.

The Choir repeats : Atténde.

1. Ad te Rex summe, ómni- um Redémptor, ó-culos nostros

sublevámus fléntes : exáudi, Christe, suppli-cántum pre-ces.
℟. Atténde.

2. Déxte-ra Patris, lapis angulá- ris, vi- a sa-lu-tis, iánu- a

cæ-lé-stis, áblu- e nostri mácu-las de-lí-cti. ℟. Atténde.

3. Rogámus, De-us, tu- am ma- iestá- tem : áuri-bus sacris gé-

mi-tus exáu-di : crími-na nostra plá-cidus indúlge. ℟.Atténde.

4. Ti-bi fa-témur crímina admís-sa : contrí-to corde pándimus

occúl-ta : tu- a, Redémptor, pí- e-tas ignóscat. ℟. Atténde.

5. Innocens captus, nec repúgnans ductus, téstibus falsis pro

ímpi- is damná- tus : quos redemí-sti, tu consérva, Chri-ste.
℟. Atténde.

152

VEXILLA REGIS

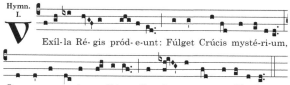

Hymn.
I.

Exíl-la Ré- gis pród- e-unt: Fúlget Crúcis mysté-ri-um,

Quo carne carnis condí-tor   Suspén- sus est pa-tí-bu-lo.

Confíxa clavis viscéra,
Tendens manus, vestígia,
Redemptiónis grátia
Hic immoláta est hóstia.

Quo vulnerátus ínsuper
Mucróne díro lánceæ,
Ut nos laváret crímine
Manávit únda Sánguine.

Impléta sunt quæ cóncinit
Dávid fidéli cármine,
Dicéndo natiónibus:
Regnávit a lígno Déus.

Arbor decóra et fúlgida
Ornáta Regis púrpura,
Elécta dígno stípite
Tam sancta mémbra tángere.

Beáta, cújus bráchiis
Prétium pepéndit sǽculi :
Statéra fácta córporis,
Prǽdam tulítque tártari.

Fundis aróma córtice,
Vincis sápore nectáre,
Jucúnda fructu fértili
Plaudis triúmpho nóbili.

Salve ara, salve víctima
De passiónis glória
Qua víta mórtem pértulit,
Et mórte vítam reddídit.

O CRUX ÀVE, SPES ÚNICA,
In hac triúmphi glória*
Auge píis justítiam
Reísque dona véniam.

Te summa, Deus, Trínitas,
Collaudet ómnis spíritus :
Quos per Crúcis mystérium
Salvas, rege per sǽcula.
Amen.

*In Passiontide:
Hoc Passiónis témpore,
In Paschal Time:
Paschále quæ fers gáudium

(Pre-1635 text)

153

Pilgrims' Songs: Chant

HYMN : VENI CREATOR SPIRITUS

Veni Creátor Spíritus, Mentes tu-órum ví-si-ta: Imple supér-na grá-ti-a Quae tu cre-ásti pécto-ra. 2. Qui Pará-clitus dí-ceris, Donum De-i al-tíssimi, Fons vivus, ignis, cá-ritas, Et spiri-tális úncti-o. 3. Tu septi-fórmis múnere, Dextræ De-i tu dí-gitus, Tu rite promíssum Patris, Sermó-ne ditans gúttura. 4. Accénde lumen sénsibus, Infùnde amó-rem córdibus, Infirma nostri córporis Virtúte firmans pér-pe-ti. 5. Hostem re-péllas lóngi-us, Pacémque dones pró-tinus: Ductóre sic te præ-ví-o, Vitémus omne nóxi-um. 6. Per te sci-àmus da Patrem, Noscàmus atque Fí-li-um, Te utri-ús-que Spi-ri-tum Credàmus omni témpore. 7. Sit laus Patri cum Fí-li-o, Sancto simul Pa-ràcli-to, Nobísque mit-tat Fí-li-us Charísma Sancti Spí-ri-tus. Amen.

154

PARCE DOMINE

Arce Dómi-ne, parce pópu-lo tu-o : ne in ætér-

num i-rascá- ris no- bis. *Repeat :* Parce Dómine.

1. Flectámus i-ram víndi-cem, Plo-rémus ante Iúdi-cem; Cla-

mémus o-re súppli-ci, Di-cámus omnes cérnu- i :

℟. Parce Dómine.

2. Nostris ma-lis offéndimus Tu- am De- us cleménti- am Ef-

fúnde no-bis désu-per Remíssor indulgénti- am.

℟. Parce Dómine.

3. Dans tempus acceptábi- le, Da lacrimárum rí-vu-lis Lavá-

re cordis víctimam, quam læta adú-rat cá-ri- tas.

℟. Parce Dómine.

4. Audi, benígne Cóndi- tor, Nostras preces cum flé-ti-bus

In hoc sacro ie-iú-ni- o Fusas quadra-gená-ri- o.

℟. Parce Dómine.

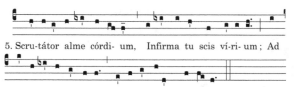

5. Scru-tátor alme córdi- um, Infirma tu scis ví-ri- um; Ad

te re-vérsis éxhi-be Remissi- o-nis grá-ti- am

℟. Parce Dómine.

AVE MARIA GRATIA

AVE Ma-rí- a, * grá-ti- a plena : Dóminus te-cum, be-

ne-dícta tu in muli- é-ribus, et benedíctus fructus ventris

tu-i, Iesus. Sancta Marí- a, Mater De- i, ora pro no-bis

pecca-tó-ribus, nunc et in ho- ra mortis nostræ. Amen.

NON NOBIS

Non— no-bis, Do- mi-ne, Do-mi-ne, non—

no-bis Do- mi- ne— sed— no-mi- ni, sed

no- mi-ni tu- o da glo-ri- am.

From Kenneth Branagh's Henry V

156

SALVE MATER MISERICORDIAE

Ⅴ. **S**alve mater mise-ri-córdi- æ, Mater De- i, et máter

véni-æ, Mater spe- i, et mater grá-ti-æ, mater plena sanctæ

læ-tí-ti- æ. O Marí- a ! *Repeat :* Salve Mater.

1. Salve, de-cus humáni géne-ris, Salve Virgo dígni-or cé-te-

ris, Quæ vírgi-nes omnes transgréde-ris, Et álti- us sédes

in sú-pe-ris, O Ma-rí- a ! *Repeat :* Salve Mater.

2. Salve fe- lix Virgo pu-érpe-ra : Nam qui sedet in Patris

déxte-ra, Cæ-lum re-gens, terram et æthe-ra, Intra tu- a

se clausit vísce-ra, O Ma-rí- a ! *Repeat :* Salve Mater.

3. Te cre-á- vit Pater ingé-ni-tus, Adamá-vit te Uni-géni-tus,

Fe-cundá-vit te sanctus Spí-ri-tus, Tu es facta to-ta di-ví-

157

ni-tus, O Ma-rí- a! *Repeat :* Salve Mater.

4. Te cre-á- vit De-us mi-rá-bi-lem, Te respé-xit ancíllam hú-

mi-lem, Te quæsí- vit spónsam amá-bi-lem, Tí- bi numquam

fé-cit consí-mi-lem, O Ma-rí- a! *Repeat :* Salve Mater.

5. Te be-á- tam laudá-re cú-pi- unt Omnes iústi, sed non suf-

fí-ci- unt ; Multas laudes de te concí-pi- unt, Sed in íl-lis

prorsus de- fí-ci- unt, O Ma-rí- a! *Repeat :* Salve Mater.

6. Esto, Ma-ter, nostrum so-lá-ti- um ; Nostrum es-to, tu Vir-

go, gáudi- um ; Et nos tandem post hoc exsí-li- um, Lætos

junge cho-ris cælésti- um, O Ma-rí- a! *Repeat :* Salve Mater.

158

THE SEVEN PENITENTIAL PSALMS

Ant.

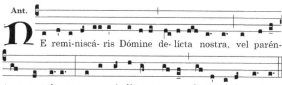

NE remi-niscá- ris Dómine de- lícta nostra, vel parén-

tum nostrórum: neque vindíctam sumas de peccá-tis nostris.

Psalmus [6]:

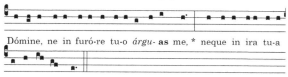

Dómine, ne in furó-re tu-o *árgu- as* me, * neque in ira tu-a

corrí-pi- **as** me.

Miserére mei, Dómine, quóni*am* in**fí**rmus sum:*
sana me, Dómine, quóniam conturbáta *sunt
ossa* **me**a.

Et ánima mea turbá*ta est* **val**de:* sed tu, *Dómine,*
úsquequo?

Convértere, Dómine, et éripe á*nimam* **me**am:* salvum me fac propter miseri*córdiam* **tu**am.

Quóniam non est in morte qui me*mor sit* **tu**i:* in
inférno autem quis confi*tébitur* **ti**bi?

Laborávi in gémitu meo, † lavábo per síngulas
noctes *lectum* **me**um:* lácrimis meis stratum
*meum ri***gá**bo.

Turbátus est a furóre ó*culus* **me**us:* inveterávi inter
omnes i*nimícos* **me**os.

Discédite a me omnes, qui operámini i*niqui***tá**tem:*
quóniam exaudívit Dóminus vo*cem fletus* **me**i.

Exaudívit Dóminus deprecati*ónem* **me**am,* Dóminus oratiónem *meam sus***cé**pit.

Erubéscant, et conturbéntur veheménter omnes inimíci **me**i:* convertántur, et erubéscant *valde*
ve**ló**citer.

Glória Pa*tri, et Fílio,** et Spirítui **San**cto.

Sicut erat in princípio, et *nunc, et semper,** et in
sǽcula sæ*culórum. A*men.

Psalmus [31]:

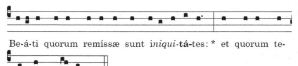

Be-á-ti quorum remíssæ sunt i*niqui*-**tá**-tes:* et quorum te-

cta sunt pec-**cá**- ta.

Beátus vir, cui non imputávit Dómi*nus pec***cá**tum,*
nec est in spíri*tu eius* **do**lus.

Quóniam tácui, inveteravérunt *ossa* **me**a,* dum
clamá*rem tota* **di**e.

Quóniam die ac nocte graváta est super me *manus*
tua:* convérsus sum in ærúmna mea, dum
con*fígitur* **spi**na.

Delíctum meum cógnitum *tibi* **fe**ci:* et iniustítiam
me*am non ab***scón**di.

Dixi: Confitébor advérsum me iniustítiam *meam*
Dómino:* et tu remisísti impietátem *peccáti*
mei.

Pro hac orábit ad te *omnis* **sanc**tus,* in tempó*re*
oppor**tú**no.

Verúmtamen in dilúvio aquá*rum mul***tá**rum,* ad
eum non *approxi***má**bunt.

Tu es refúgium meum a tribulatióne, quæ circúmdedit me:* exsultátio mea, érue me a circumdántibus me.

Intelléctum tibi dabo, et ínstruam te in via hac, qua gradiéris:* firmábo super te óculos meos.

Nolíte fíeri sicut equus et mulus,* quibus non est intelléctus.

In camo et freno maxíllas eórum constrínge,* qui non appróximant ad te.

Multa flagélla peccatóris,* sperántem autem in Dómino misericórdia circúmdábit.

Lætámini in Dómino et exsultáte iusti,* et gloriámini omnes recti corde.

Glória Patri.

Psalmus [37]:

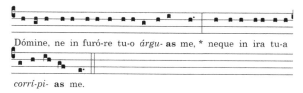

Dómine, ne in furó-re tu-o árgu- as me, * neque in ira tu-a

corrí-pi- as me.

Quóniam sagíttæ tuæ infíxæ sunt mihi:* et confirmásti super me manum tuam.

Non est sánitas in carne mea a fácie iræ tuæ:* non est pax óssibus meis a fácie peccatórum meórum.

Quóniam iniquitátes meæ supergréssæ sunt caput meum:* et sicut onus grave gravátæ sunt super me.

Putruérunt et corrúptæ sunt cicatríces meæ,* a fácie insipiéntiæ meæ.

Miser factus sum, et curvátus sum us*que in* **fi**nem:*
tota die contristátus *ingredi*ébar.

Quóniam lumbi mei impléti sunt il*lusi*ónibus:* et
non est sánitas *in carne* **me**a.

Afflíctus sum, et humiliá*tus sum* **ni**mis:* rugiébam
a gémi*tu cordis* **me**i.

Dómine, ante te omne desidé*rium* **me**um:* et gémitus meus a te *non est ab***scónd**itus.

Cor meum conturbátum est, † derelíquit me *virtus*
mea:* et lumen oculórum meórum, et ip*sum*
non est **me**cum.

Amíci mei, et pró*ximi* **me**i:* advérsum me ap-
propinquavé*runt, et ste***té**runt.

Et qui iuxta me erant, de lon*ge ste***té**runt:* et vim
faciébant qui quærébant *ánimam* **me**am.

Et qui inquirébant mala mihi, locúti sunt *vani***tá**tes:*
et dolos tota die *medita***bán**tur.

Ego autem tamquam surdus non *audi*ébam:* et sicut
mutus non apé*riens os* **su**um.

Et factus sum sicut ho*mo non* **áu**diens:* et non
habens in ore suo re*darguti*ónes.

Quóniam in te, Dómi*ne, spe***rá**vi:* tu exaúdies me,
Dómi*ne, Deus* **me**us.

Quia dixi: Ne quando supergaúdeant mihi ini*míci*
mei:* et dum commovéntur pedes mei, super
me *magna lo***cú**ti sunt.

Quóniam ego in flagél*la pa***rá**tus sum:* et dolor
meus in conspéc*tu meo* **sem**per.

Quóniam iniquitátem meam an*nunti***á**bo:* et cogi-
tábo pro *peccáto* **me**o.

Inimíci autem mei vivunt, et confirmá*ti sunt* **super**
me:* et multiplicáti sunt qui odé*runt me in***í**que.

Qui retríbuunt mala pro bonis, detra*hébant* **mi**hi:*
quóniam sequé*bar boni*tátem.

Ne derelínquas me, Dómine, *Deus* **me**us:* ne
dis*césseris* **a** me.

Inténde in adiutó*rium* **me**um,* Dómine, Deus
salútis **me**æ.

Glória Patri.

Psalmus [50]:

Mi-se-ré-re *me- i*, **De**-us, * secúndum magnam mise-ri- *córdi-*
am **tu**- am.

Et secúndum multitúdinem miseratió*num tu*árum,*
dele ini*quitátem* **me**am.

Ámplius lava me ab iniqui*táte* **me**a:* et a peccá*to
meo* **munda** me.

Quóniam iniquitátem meam e*go co*g**nó**sco:* et pec-
cátum meum con*tra me est* **sem**per.

Tibi soli peccávi, et malum co*ram te* **fe**ci:* ut iusti-
ficéris in sermónibus tuis, et vincas *cum iu-
di*cá*ris.

Ecce enim in iniquitáti*bus con*c**ép**tus sum:* et in
peccátis concépit *me mater* **me**a.

Ecce enim veritátem *dile*xísti:* incérta et occúlta
sapiéntiæ tuæ mani*festásti* **mi**hi.

Aspérges me hyssópo, *et mun*dábor:* lavábis me, et
super niv*em deal*bábor.

Audítui meo dabis gaúdium, *et lætí*tiam:* et
  exsultábunt ossa *humili*áta.

Avérte fáciem tuam a pec*cátis* **me**is:* et omnes in-
  iquitá*tes meas* **de**le.

Cor mundum crea *in me,* **De**us:* et spíritum rectum
  ínnova in vis*céribus* **me**is.

Ne proícias me a fá*cie* **tu**a:* et Spíritum sanctum
  tuum ne *áuferas* **a** me.

Redde mihi lætítiam salu*táris* **tu**i:* et spíritu prin-
  ci*páli con*fírma me.

Docébo iníquos *vias* **tu**as:* et ímpii ad *te conver-*
  téntur.

Líbera me de sanguínibus, Deus, Deus sa*lútis*
  meæ:* et exsultábit lingua mea ius*títiam* **tu**am.

Dómine, lábia me*a a*péries:* et os meum annun-
  tiá*bit laudem* **tu**am.

Quóniam si voluísses sacrifícium, de*díssem*
  útique:* holocaústis *non delec*táberis.

Sacrifícium Deo spíritus con*tribu*látus:* cor con-
  trítum et humiliátum, De*us, non de*spície*s.

Benígne fac, Dómine, in bona voluntáte *tua* **Si**on:*
  ut ædificéntur *muri* **Ie**rúsalem.

Tunc acceptábis sacrifícium iustítiæ, oblatiónes, et
  *holo*cáusta:* tunc inpónent super altá*re tuum*
  vítulos.

Glória Patri.

Psalmus [101]:

Dómine, exaudi orati- *ó-nem* **me**-am: * et clamor me- *us ad*

te **vé-ni-** at.

Non avértas fáciem *tuam* **a** me:* in quacúmque die
tríbulor, inclína ad *me aurem* **tu**am.

In quacúmque die invo*cáve*ro te,* velóc*iter ex***áudi**
me.

Quia defecérunt sicut fumus *dies* **me**i:* et ossa mea
sicut crémi*um aru***é**runt.

Percússus sum ut fænum, et áru*it cor* **me**um:* quia
oblítus sum coméd*ere panem* **me**um.

A voce gém*itus* **me**i* adhæsit os me*um carni* **me**æ.

Símilis factus sum pelicáno *soli***tú**dinis: *factus sum
sicut nyctícorax *in domi***cíli**o.

*Vigi***lá**vi,* et factus sum sicut passer solitá*rius in*
tecto.

Tota die exprobrábant mihi inim*íci* **me**i:* et qui
laudábant me, advér*sum me iu***rá**bant.

Quia cínerem tamquam panem *mandu***cá**bam,* et
potum meum cum *fletu mi***scé**bam.

A fácie iræ et indignatió*nis* **tu**æ:* quia éle*vans al-
li***sísti** me.

Dies mei sicut umbra de*clina***vé**runt:* et ego si*cut
fænum* **aru**i.

Tu autem, Dómine, in æt*érnum* **pér**manes:* et
memoriále tuum in generatióne et ge*neratió-*
nem.

Tu exsúrgens miser*éberis* **Si**on:* quia tempus
miseréndi eius, qui*a venit* **tem**pus.

165

Quóniam placuérunt servis tuis lá*pides* eius:* et
terræ eius *misere***bún**tur.

Et timébunt Gentes nomen *tuum,* **Dómine,*** et omnes reges terræ *glóriam* **tu**am.

Quia ædificávit Dó*minus* **Sion:*** et vidébitur in *glória* **su**a.

Respéxit in oratió*nem hu***mí**lium:* et non sprevit
*precem e***ó**rum.

Scribántur hæc in generati*óne* **ál**tera:* et pópulus,
qui creábitur, *laudábit* **Dómin**um:

Quia prospéxit de excélso *sancto* **su**o:* Dóminus de
cælo in *terram a***spé**xit:

Ut audíret gémitus com*pedi***tó**rum:* ut sólvéret
fílios *interem***pt**órum:

Ut annúntient in Sion *nomen* **Dó**mini:* et laudem
ei*us in Ie***rúsa**lem.

In conveniéndo pópu*los in* **u**num,* et reges ut *sérvi-
ant* **Dómi**no.

Respóndit ei in via vir*tútis* **su**æ:* Paucitátem diérum meórum *núntia* **mi**hi.

Ne révoces me in dimídio dié*rum me***ó**rum:* in gen-
eratiónem et generatió*nem anni* **tu**i.

Inítio tu, Dómine, ter*ram fun***dá**sti:* et opera mánuum tu*árum sunt* **cæ**li.

Ipsi períbunt, tu *autem* **pér**manes:* et omnes sicut
vestimén*tum vete***rá**scent.

Et sicut opertórium mutábis eos, et *mutabún*tur:* tu
autem idem ipse es, et anni tu*i non de***fí**cient.

Fílii servórum tuórum *habi***tá**bunt:* et semen eórum
in sæcu*lum diri***gé**tur.

Glória Patri.

Psalmus [129]:

De pro-fúndis clamávi *ad te,* **Dómi**-ne: * Dómine, exáu-*di*

vo- cem **me**- am.

Fiant aures tuæ *intén***dén**tes,* in vocem depre-
ca**tiónis me**æ.

Si iniquitátes observá*veris,* **Dómine:*** Dómine, *quis
susti***né**bit?

Quia apud te propiti*átio* est:* et propter legem tuam
sust*ínui te,* **Dóm**ine.

Sust*ínuit ánima mea in *verbo* **e**ius:* sperávit ánima
mea in **Dóm**ino.

A custódia matutína us*que ad* **n**octem,* speret
Ís*raël in* **Dóm**ino.

Quia apud Dóminum mi*seri***cór**dia:* et copióosa
apud *eum re***démpti**o.

Et ipse ré*dimet* **I**sraël,* ex ómnibus iniqui*tátibus*
eius.

Glória Patri.

Psalmus [142]:

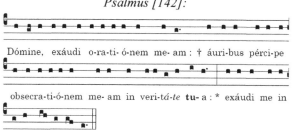

Dómine, exáudi o-ra-ti-ó-nem me- am : † áuri-bus pérci-pe

obsecra-ti-ó-nem me- am in veri-*tá-te* **tu**- a : * exáudi me in

tu- a iu**sti**- ti- a.

Et non intres in iudícium cum *servo* **tu**o:* quia non
iustificábitur in conspéctu tu*o omnis* **v**ivens.

Quia persecútus est inimícus á*nimam* **me**am:* hu-
miliávit in ter*ra vitam* **me**am.

Collocávit me in obscúris sicut mór*tuos* **sǽ**culi:* et
anxiátus est super me spíritus meus, in me turbá*tum est cor* **me**um.

Memor fui diérum antiquórum, † meditátus sum in
ómnibus opé*ribus* **tu**is:* in factis manuum
tuá*rum medi***tá**bar.

Expándi manus *meas* **ad** te:* ánima mea sicut terra
si*ne aqua* **ti**bi.

Velóciter exáu*di me,* **Dó**mine:* defecit *spíritus*
meus.

Non avértas fáciem *tuam* **a** me:* et símilis ero
descendén*tibus in* **la**cum.

Audítam fac mihi mane misericór*diam* **tu**am:* quia
in te spe**rá**vi.

Notam fac mihi viam, *in qua* **ám**bulem:* quia ad te
levávi *ánimam* **me**am.

Éripe me de inimícis meis, Dómine, ad *te con***fú**gi:*
doce me fácere voluntátem tuam, quia De*us*
meus **es** tu.

Spíritus tuus bonus dedúcet me in *terram* **re**ctam:*
propter nomen tuum, Dómine, vivificábis me,
in æ*quitáte* **tu**a.

Edúces de tribulatióne *ánimam* **me**am:* et in misericórdia tua dispérdes i*nimícos* **me**os.

Et perdes omnes, qui tríbulant *ánimam* **me**am:*
quóniam e*go servus* **tuus** sum.

Glória Patri.

Antiphon is repeated: p157.

HYMN: AVE MARIS STELLA

A-ve ma-ris stella, De- i Mater alma, Atque sem-

per Virgo, Fe-lix cæ-li porta. 2. Sumens illud Ave Ga-

bri- é- lis o- re, Funda nos in pace, Mutans Hevæ nomen.

3. Solve vincla re- is, Pro-fer lumen cæ-cis : Ma-la nostra

pelle, Bona cuncta posce. 4. Monstra *te* esse matrem : Su-

mat per te pre-ces, Qui pro nobis natus Tu-lit esse tu-us.

5. Virgo singulá-ris, Inter omnes mi- tis, Nos culpis so-lu-

tos, Mi-tes fac et castos. 6. Vitam præsta puram, I-ter

para tu-tum: Ut vidéntes Iesum, Semper collæ-témur. 7. Sit

laus De- o Patri, Summo Christo de-cus, Spi-rí-tu- i San-

cto. Tri-bus honor unus. Amen.

Magnificat & Iubilate canons

Ma - gni-fi - cat,_____ ma - gni - fi - cat

a - ni - ma me - a,

can - ta - te,_____ can - ta - te

Do - mi - no. Glo - ri - a.

Al - le - lu - ia, al - le - lu - ia,

sem - - per.

Iu - bi - la - te De - o,

iu - bi - la - te De - o.

Al - le - lu - ia.

ENGLISH HYMNS

TRADITIONAL CATHOLIC HYMNS

FAITH OF OUR FATHERS
Key: D major; Starting note: D; Tune: Sawston

Faith of our fathers, living still,
In spite of dungeon, fire and sword;
O how our hearts beat high with joy
Whenever we hear that glorious word!

Faith of our fathers, holy faith!
We will be true to thee till death.
We will be true to thee till death.

Our fathers, chained in prisons dark,
Were still in heart and conscience free:
How sweet would be their children's fate,
If they, like them, could die for thee!

Faith of our fathers, Mary's prayers
Shall win our country back to thee;
And through the truth that comes from God
England shall then indeed be free.

Faith of our fathers, we will love
Both friend and foe in all our strife,
And preach thee, too, as love knows how
By kindly words and virtuous life:

Fr Frederick Faber, 1849

SONG OF THE ENGLISH ZOUAVES,
1860-1870

St. George and old Eng - land for ev - er!

Once more her sons___ arm for the fight.

With the Cross on the breasts, to do bat - tle

for God, Ho - ly Church and the right.

Twine your swords with the palm branch,

brave com - - - rades,

For as pil - grims we march forth to - day:___

Love God, O my soul love Him on -

ly, and then with light heart go thy way.

We come from the blue shores of England,
From the mountains of Scotia we come,
From the green, faithful island of Erin, —
Far, far, from our wild northern home.
Place Saint Andrew's white cross in your bonnets,
Saint Patrick's green shamrock display ; —
Love God, O my soul, love him only.
And then with light heart go thy way.

Dishonour our swords shall not tarnish,
We draw them for Rome and the Pope ;
Victors still, whether living or dying,
For the Martyr's bright crown is our hope ;
If 'tis sweet for our country to perish.
Sweeter far for the cause of today ; —
Love God, O my soul, love him only.
And then with light heart go thy way.

Though the odds be against us, what matter
While God and Our Lady look down.
And the Saints of our country are near us.
And Angels are holding the crown.
March, march to the combat and fear not,
A light round our weapons will play ; —
Love God, O my soul, love him only.
And then with light heart go thy way.

Recorded by Joseph Powell:
Two Years in the Pontifical Zouaves 1871
Music by Colin Mawby.

GOD BLESS OUR POPE
Key: G major; Starting note: D

Full in the panting heart of Rome
Beneath the Apostle's crowning dome.
From pilgrims' lips that kiss the ground,
Breathes in all tongues one only sound:

*God bless our Pope, God bless our Pope,
God bless our Pope, the great, the good!*

The golden roof, the marble walls,
The Vatican's majestic halls,
The note redoubles, till it fills
With echoes sweet the seven hills:

Then surging through each hallowed gate,
Where martyr Saints, in peace await
It sweeps beyond the solemn plain,
Peals over Alps, across the main:

From torrid south to frozen north,
The wave harmonious stretches forth,
Yet strikes no chord more true to Rome's,
Than rings within our hearts and homes:

For like the sparks of unseen fire,
That speak along the magic wire,
From home to home, from heart to heart,
These words of countless children dart:

Nicholas, Cardinal Wiseman, 1878

HAIL, GLORIOUS SAINT PATRICK

Hail, glo-rious Saint Pat-rick, dear Saint of our Isle!

On us, thy poor chil-dren, be-stow a sweet smile;

And now thou art high in the man-sions a-bove,

On E-rin's green val-leys look down in thy love,

On E-rin's green val-leys, On E-rin's green val-leys,

On E-rin's green val-leys look down in thy love!

Hail, glorious Saint Patrick, thy words were once
   strong
Against Satan's wiles and an infidel throng;
Not less is thy might where in heaven thou art;
O, come to our aid, in our battle take part.
O, come to our aid, O, come to our aid,
O, come to our aid, in our battle take part.

In the war against sin, in the fight for the faith,
Dear saint, may thy children resist unto death;
May their strength be in meekness, in penance, their
   prayer,
Their banner the cross which they glory to bear.
Their banner the cross, their banner the cross,.
Their banner the cross which they glory to bear.

Thy people, now exiles on many a shore,
Shall love and revere thee till time be no more;

And the fire thou hast kindled shall ever burn bright,
Its warmth undiminished, undying its light.
Its warmth undiminished, its warmth undiminished,
Its warmth undiminished, undying its light.

Ever bless and defend the sweet land of our birth,
Where the shamrock still blooms as when thou wert
    on earth,
And our hearts shall yet burn, wherever we roam,
For God and Saint Patrick, and our native home.
For God and Saint Patrick, for God and Saint Patrick,
For God and Saint Patrick, and our native home.

Sister Agnes, 1920;
music by Henry Hemy (1818-1888)

HYMN OF ST EDMUND'S COLLEGE, WARE

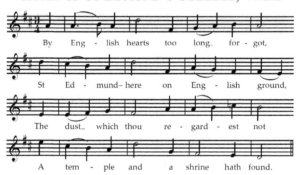

By   Eng - lish   hearts   too   long   for - got,

St   Ed - mund— here   on   Eng - lish   ground,

The   dust— which   thou   re - gard - est   not

A   tem - ple   and   a   shrine   hath   found.

Whose age so spent, whose death so died
A pilgrimage thy world confessed,
By alien welcome fortified,
By alien mourners laid to rest.

Long years, to wait the last great morn,
Thy body slept its homeless sleep,
Till England's faith from England torn
Bade martyrs bleed and Angels weep.

176

St Alban's home, St Thomas's shrine
Did sacrilegious hands o'erthrow,
And shepherds of a faith not thine
Mis-led thy flock of long ago.

Lovers of faith and country then
Thy footsteps followed oversea,
And rather serving God than men,
By exile hastened to be free.

Thence one by one, in guileless fraud,
Returned to brave the tyrant's will,
Their Master, with themselves outlawed,
To hungry souls restoring still.

Outlaws they lived, that exiles were,
Hermits they walked by ways unknown,
A prey to every traitor's snare,
Unfriended friends of faith o'erthrown.

Dungeons their home, the rack their bed,
A hurdle at the long day's end,
With thee at last they found instead
The sleep no pillow here could lend.

To freedom and to home restored,
Our fathers from their exile came,
And built this house on English sward,
Father of exiles, in thy name.

Father, in heaven employ thy prayer,
Lest we, whom happier times befriend,
Forgetful of our birthright there,
On this dull world our love should spend.

O God, whom welcomed Saints adore,
In Substance One, in Persons Three,
Grant that our hearts, like theirs before,
No rest may know, save only in thee.

Mgr R.A. Knox;
music by John Richardson (1819-1879)

Help of Christians

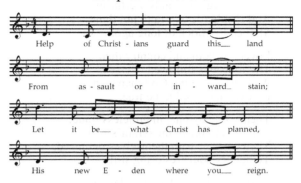

Help of Christ - ians guard this__ land
From as - sault or in - ward__ stain;
Let it be__ what Christ has planned,
His new E - den where you__ reign.

Teach us that in Christ your Son
Lies the wisdom to be free;
For the cross which we would shun
Is Man's tree of liberty.

Should the powers of hell arise
And our peace be trampled down,
In that night of blood and lies
Show us still your twelve starred crown.

Take from us the coward heart,
Fleeting will, divided mind;
Give us sight to play our part
Though the world around is blind.

Image of the risen life
Shining in eternity,
Glimmer through our earthly strife,
Draw us to your victory.

James McAuley (1917-1976);
music by Richard Connolly (b1927)

HAIL REDEEMER, KING DIVINE
Key: G; starting note: G.

Hail Redeemer, King divine!
Priest and Lamb, the throne is thine;
King, whose reign shall never cease,
Prince of everlasting peace.

Angels, saints and nations sing :
"Praise be Jesus Christ our King;
Lord of life, earth, sky and sea,
King of love on Calvary!"

King most holy, King of truth,
Guard the lowly, guide the youth;
Christ the King of glory bright,
Be to us eternal light.

Shepherd-king, o'er mountains steep
Homeward bring the wandering sheep;
Shelter in one royal fold
States and kingdoms, new and old.

Crimson streams, O King of grace,
Drenched thy thorn-crowned head and face;
Floods of love's redeeming tide
Tore thy hands, thy feet, and side.

Eucharistic King, what love
Draws thee daily from above,
Clad in signs of bread and wine :
Feed us, lead us, keep us thine!

King, whose name creation thrills,
Rule our hearts, our minds, our wills;
Till in peace, each nation rings
With thy praises, King of kings.

Sing with joy in ev'ry home :
"Christ our King, thy kingdom come!
To the King of ages, then,
Honour, glory, love : Amen!"

Fr Patrick Brennan, 1940

BE THOU MY VISION
Key: E flat; starting note: E flat

Be thou my Vision, O Lord of my heart;
Naught be all else to me, save that thou art
Thou my best thought, by day or by night,
Waking or sleeping, thy presence my light.

Be thou my Wisdom, and thou my true Word;
I ever with thee and thou with me, Lord;
Thou my great Father and I thy true son;
Thou in me dwelling, and I with thee one.

Be thou my battle Shield, Sword for the fight;
Be thou my dignity, thou my Delight;
Thou my soul's Shelter, and thou my high Tower:
Raise thou me heavenward, O Power of my power.

Riches I heed not, nor man's empty praise,
Thou mine Inheritance, now and always:
Thou and thou only, the first in my heart,
High King of Heaven, my Treasure thou art.

High King of Heaven, my victory won,
May I reach Heaven's joys, O bright Heaven's Sun!
Heart of my own heart, whatever befall,
Still be my Vision, O Ruler of all.

Translated from a 6th Century Irish original,
this version by Eleanor Hull, 1912

O GOD OF EARTH AND ALTAR

O God of earth and al - tar,

Bow down and hear our cry,

Our earth - ly rul - ers fal - ter,

Our peo - ple drift and die;

The walls of gold en - tomb us,

The swords of scorn di - vide,

Take not thy thun - der from us,

But take a - way our pride.

From all that terror teaches,
from lies of tongue and pen,
from all the easy speeches
that comfort cruel men,
from sale and profanation
of honour, and the sword,
from sleep and from damnation,
deliver us, good Lord!

Tie in a living tether
the prince and priest and thrall,
bind all our lives together,
smite us and save us all;
in ire and exultation
aflame with faith, and free,
lift up a living nation,
a single sword to thee.

G.K. Chesterton, 1906

SOUL OF MY SAVIOUR
Key: G major; starting note: D

Soul of my Saviour sanctify my breast,
Body of Christ, be thou my saving guest,
Blood of my Saviour, bathe me in thy tide,
wash me with waters gushing from thy side.

Strength and protection may thy passion be,
O blessed Jesus, hear and answer me;
Deep in thy wounds, Lord, hide and shelter me,
So shall I never, never part from thee.

Guard and defend me from the foe malign,
In death's dread moments make me only thine;
Call me and bid me come to thee on high
Where I may praise thee with thy saints for ay.

Anima Christi (see pp129) *trans. J. Hegarty*

BL. JOHN HENRY, CARDINAL NEWMAN'S HYMNS

FIRMLY I BELIEVE AND TRULY

Firm - ly I be - lieve and tru - ly
God is Three and God is one;
and I next ac - know - ledge du - ly
man - hood tak - en by the Son.

And I trust and hope most fully
In that Manhood crucified;
And each thought and deed unruly
Do to death, as he has died.

Simply to his grace and wholly
Light and life and strength belong,
And I love supremely, solely,
Him the holy, him the strong.

And I hold in veneration,
For the love of him alone,
Holy Church as his creation,
And her teachings as his own.

And I take with joy whatever
Now besets me, pain or fear,
And with a strong will I sever
All the ties which bind me here.

Adoration aye be given,
With and through th' angelic host,
To the God of earth and Heaven,
Father, Son and Holy Ghost.

1865

LEAD KINDLY LIGHT

Lead kind-ly light, a - mid th'en-circ-ling gloom,
Lead thou me on. The night is dark,
and I am far from home; Lead thou me on.
Keep thou my feet; I do not ask to see the
dis - tant scene; one step e - nough for me.

I was not ever thus, nor prayed that thou
    shouldst lead me on;
I loved to choose and see my path; but now
    lead thou me on!
I loved the garish day, and, spite of fears,
Pride ruled my will. Remember not past years!

So long thy power hath blest me, sure it still
    will lead me on.
O'er moor and fen, o'er crag and torrent, till
    the night is gone,
And with the morn those angel faces smile,
Which I have loved long since, and lost awhile!

Meantime, along the narrow rugged path,
    thyself hast trod,
Lead, Saviour, lead me home in childlike faith,
    home to my God.
To rest forever after earthly strife
In the calm light of everlasting life.   *1833*

PRAISE TO THE HOLIEST
Key: A flat major; starting note: C

Praise to the Holiest in the height,
And in the depth be praise;
In all his words most wonderful,
Most sure in all his ways.

O loving wisdom of our God!
When all was sin and shame,
A second Adam to the fight
And to the rescue came.

O wisest love! that flesh and blood,
Which did in Adam fail,
Should strive afresh against the foe,
Should strive and should prevail.

And that a higher gift than grace
Should flesh and blood refine,
God's Presence and his very Self,
And Essence all divine.

O generous love! that he, who smote,
In Man for man the foe,
The double agony in Man
For man should undergo.

And in the garden secretly,
And on the Cross on high,
Should teach his brethren, and inspire
To suffer and to die.

Praise to the Holiest in the height,
And in the depth be praise;
In all his words most wonderful,
Most sure in all his ways.

1865

MARIAN HYMNS

MEMORARE
Key: F major; starting note: A

O Mother blest, whom God bestows
On sinners and on just,
What joy, what hope thou givest those
Who in thy mercy trust.

Thou art clement, thou art chaste,
Mary, thou art fair;
Of all mothers sweetest, best,
None with thee compare.

O heavenly Mother, mistress sweet!
It never yet was told
That suppliant sinner left thy feet
Unpitied, unconsoled.

O Mother, pitiful and mild,
Cease not to pray for me;
For I do love thee as a child,
And sigh for love of thee.

Most powerful Mother, all men know
Thy Son denies thee nought;
Thou askest, wishest it, and lo!
His power thy will hath wrought.

O Mother blest, for me obtain,
Ungrateful though I be,
To love that God who first could deign
To show such love for me.

St. Alphonsus (1696-1787),
trans: E. Vaughan, 1844

HAIL QUEEN OF HEAVEN
Key: G major; starting note: B

Hail, Queen of heaven, the ocean star,
Guide of the wanderer here below,
Thrown on life's surge, we claim thy care,
Save us from peril and from woe.

Mother of Christ, Star of the sea
Pray for the wanderer, pray for me.

O gentle, chaste, and spotless Maid,
We sinners make our prayers through thee;
Remind thy Son that he has paid
The price of our iniquity.

Virgin most pure, Star of the sea,
Pray for the sinner, pray for me.

Sojourners in this vale of tears,
Blest advocate, to thee we cry,
Assuage our sorrows, calm our fears,
And soothe with hope our misery.

Refuge in grief, Star of the sea
Pray for the mourner, pray for me.

And while to him who reigns above
In Godhead one, in Persons three,
The Source of life, of grace, of love,
Homage we pay on bended knee:

Do thou, bright Queen, Star of the sea,
Pray for thy children, pray for me.

Fr John Lingard, 1851

O PUREST OF CREATURES
Key: G major; starting note: D

O purest of creatures, sweet Mother, sweet Maid,
The one spotless womb wherein Jesus was laid,
Dark night hath come down on us, Mother, and we
Look out for thy shining, sweet Star of the Sea.

Deep night hath come down on this rough-spoken
world,
And the banners of darkness are boldly unfurled:
And the tempest-tossed Church all her eyes are on
thee,
They look to thy shining, sweet Star of the Sea.

He gazed on thy soul; it was spotless and fair;
For the empire of sin—it hath never been there;
None had e'er owned thee, dear Mother, but he,
And he blessed thy clear shining, sweet Star of the
Sea!

Earth gave him one lodging: 'twas deep in thy
breast,
And God found a home where the sinner finds rest;
His home and his hiding-place, both were in thee;
He was won by thy shining, sweet Star of the Sea.

Oh, blissful and calm was the wonderful rest
That thou gavest thy God in thy Virginal breast;
For the heaven he left he found heaven in thee,
And he shone with thy shining, sweet Star of the
Sea.

Fr Frederick Faber

IMMACULATE MARY (the Lourdes Hymn)
Key: F major; starting note: C

Immaculate Mary! / Our hearts are on fire,
That title so wondrous / Fills all our desire.

Ave, ave, ave Maria! / Ave, ave, ave Maria!

We pray for God's glory, / The Lord's kingdom
    come!
We pray for his vicar, / Our Father, and Rome.

We pray for our Mother / The Church upon earth,
And bless, sweetest Lady, / The land of our birth.

O Mary! O Mother! / Reign o'er us once more;
Be England thy Dowry / As in days of yore.

We pray for all sinners / And souls that now stray
From Jesus and Mary / In heresy's way.

For poor, sick, afflicted / Thy mercy we crave;
And comfort the dying / Thou light of the grave.

There is no need, Mary, / Nor ever has been,
Which thou canst not succour, / Immaculate Queen.

In grief and temptation, / In joy or in pain,
We'll ask thee, our mother, / Nor seek thee in vain.

O bless us, dear Lady, / With blessings from heav-
    en.
And to our petitions / Let answer be given.

In death's solemn moment, / Our mother, be nigh;
As children of Mary — / O teach us to die.

And crown thy sweet mercy / With this special
    grace,
To behold soon in heaven / God's ravishing face.

To God be all glory / And worship for aye,
And to God's Virgin Mother / An endless Ave.

Abbé Gaignet of Lucon; trans anon, 1900

Walsingham Hymns

THE WALSINGHAM HYMN
Key: F major; starting note: C

All **glory** to God in his mercy *and* grace,
Who hath es**tab**lish'd his Home in this wonder*ful* place.

Ave Ave Ave Maria! Ave Ave Ave Maria!

All **glory** to Jesus our Saviour *and* Lord,
Whose **im**age within us by grace is *res*tor'd.

All **glory** to God in his Spirit *Di*vine.
Who hath **fix'd** his abode in this poor soul *of* mine.

Sing the **prai**ses of Mary, the Mother *of* God,
Whose '**Wal**singham Way' countless pilgrims *have* trod.

Then **lift** high your voices, rehearse the *glad* tale,
Of Our **La**dy's appearing in Stiffkey's *fair* vale.

When **Ed**ward Confessor rul'd over *the* land,
The **Fa**verches' Manor stood here nigh *at* hand.

The **La**dy Richeldis devoted *her* care,
To **good** works and penance and worship *and* prayer.

One **day** as she pray'd and look'd up to *the* skies,
A **vis**ion of splendour delighted *her* eyes.

Our **La**dy, God's Mother, in glory *ar*ray'd,
Held a **House** in her arms which was clearly **dis**play'd.

'Take **note**, my dear daughter, and build here *a* Shrine
As **Na**zareth's home in this country *of* thine.'

'And the **spot** that I choose where the house shall *ar*ise
By a **sign** shall be plainly reveal'd to *thine* eyes.'

The **vi**sion pass'd slowly away from *her* sight,
But her **mind** held the House in its length, breadth *and*
    height.

Bewi**lder**'d she ponder'd this message *so* sweet,
When a **clear** spring of water burst forth at *her* feet.

Bewi**lder**'d no longer, for this was *the* sign,
She **vow'd** on this spot she would build such *a* shrine.

The **fi**nest materials her workmen *could* find
She em**ploy'd** for this House she had fix'd in *her* mind

But **though** she had given both timbers *and* lands,
The **pow'r** of the work lay in Mary's *own* hands.

And **this** was made clear when the work was *com*plete
By th' **an**swers to prayers pour'd out at *her* feet.

And **soon** mighty wonders by grace were *re*veal'd,
For the **sick** who made use of the waters *were* heal'd.

So **Wal**singham then came a place of *great* fame,
And Our **La**dy herself was call'd by *this* name.

And **ma**ny a pilgrim to the day of *his* death
Took the **road** once a year to 'England's Na*za*reth.'

So **crowd'd** were roads that the stars, peo*ple* say,
That **shine** in the heavens were call'd 'Wal*singham*
    Way.'

And **ma**ny the favours and graces *be*stow'd,
On **those** who in faith took the pilgri*mage* road.

The **Image** of Mary with her Ho*ly* Son
Was **ho**nour'd and feted by ev-*ery*one.

The **Ca**nons and Friars built houses *ar*ound,
And the **prai**ses of God were a regu*lar* sound.

And **Kings**, Lords and commons their homage *would* pay,
And the **bur**ning of tapers turn'd night in*to* day.

But at **last** came a King who had greed in *his* eyes,
And he **lust'd** for treasure with fraud and *with* lies.

The **or**der went forth; and with horror *'twas* learn'd,
That the **Shrine** was destroy'd and the Image *was* burn'd.

And **here** where God's Mother had once been *en*thron'd,
The **souls** that stay'd faithful 'neath tyran*ny* groan'd.

And this **realm** which had once been Our Lady's *own*
      Dower,
Had its **Church** now enslav'd by the secu*lar* power.

And **so** dark night fell on this glori*ous* place,
Where of **all** former glories there hardly *was* trace.

Yet a **thin** stream of pilgrims still walk'd the *old* way,
And **hearts** long'd to see this night turn'd in*to* day.

Till at **last**, when full measure of penance *was* pour'd,
In her **Shrine** see the honour of Mary *res*tor'd:

Again '**neath** her Image the tapers *shine* fair,
In her **chil**dren's endeavours past wrongs to *re*pair.

Ag**ain** in her House her due honour *is* taught:
Her **name** is invok'd, her fair graces *be*sought:

And the **sick** and the maim'd seek the pilgri*mage* way,
And mir**a**culous healing their bodies *dis*play.

Oh **Mo**ther, give heed to the prayer of *our* heart,
That your **glo**ry from here never more may *de*part.

Now to **God** the All-Father and Son, with *due* praise,
And **life**-giving Spirit, thanksgiving *we* raise.

Anon.

MARY OF WALSINGHAM

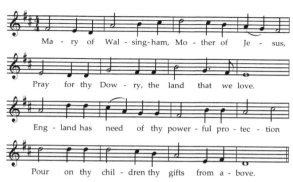

Ma - ry of Wal - sing-ham, Mo - ther of Je - sus,
Pray for thy Dow - ry, the land that we love.
Eng - land has need of thy power - ful pro - tec - tion
Pour on thy chil - dren thy gifts from a - bove.

Thou who didst summon thy servant Richeldis,
Bidding her build to thine honour a shrine,
Help us to follow in thy blesséd footsteps,
Framing our lives on thy pattern divine.

Countless the pilgrims whose footsteps have echo'd
Down through the years along Walsingham Way.
Countless the prayers that thy children have offer'd
Mary of Walsingham hear us we pray.

Many long years saw thy image neglected,
Only a few sought the help of thy prayers:
Walsingham's Shrine now again in its beauty
Welcomes each pilgrim who thither repairs.

Pray for us then, blessed Mary, our Mother,
Pray for thy children who kneel in thy shrine.
Pray that thy Son upon England thy Dowry
Pour down his favours and blessings divine.

So shall we praise thee with ceaseless thanksgiving,
So shall we sing of thy love and thy power.
So shall we feel thy protection and comfort,
All though our lives and in death's solemn hour.

Anon; music by Joseph Thrupp (1827-1867)

Our Lady of Walsingham

Here journ-eyed, on the Pil-grims' Way,

With Christ-en-dom in youth and flower,

The faith-ful of a hap-pier day

When all the land was Ma-ry's dower.

And aft-er many a faith-less year,

Since not in vain the mar-tyrs sowed,

We, as God wills, to wor-ship here

Re - turn a - long the an-cient road.

Once more with invocation due,
Lady, thy solemn names ascend,
While for thy prayer we ask anew
To guard our days and bless our end.
Maiden most humble, angels' Queen,
Mother and handmaid of the Lord,
Of God's design the goal foreseen,
Fountain of hope and love's reward:

Thou, by the grace of God thy Son
Our pillar and our ground of grace,
Perfect in us the work begun
And sanctify the rescu'd race.
In worldly storm, in stress of ill,
Be thou the star that lights our sea;
Keep us in courage, set our will
And guide us whither we would be.

Mistress of Truth in depth and height,
Good Counsel's mother, Wisdom's throne,
Teach us by light to gaze on light
Till we shall know as we are known.
So prayed our fathers at thy feet,
So hailed thee at the selfsame shrine,
And knew no mother's name so sweet
Nor any home so dear as thine.

We, coming by the way they came,
Confessing that which they confessed,
In their communion bless the name
To every generation blessed.
With theirs and ours thy voice be one,
Thou, under God exalted most,
Adoring always with the Son,
The Father and the Holy Ghost.

Walter Shewring (1938)

HAIL MARY, EVER BLESSED,

Hail Ma - ry,— e - ver bles - séd,
of Wal - sing - ham the Queen.
Through vi - sion— of Rich - el - dis,
thy fav - ours there were seen,
When Eng - land was thy dow - ry,
there— pil - grims bow'd the knee,
At morn and— noon and e - ven,
they knelt— to hon - our thee.

Hail Mary, ever blessed, thy children still delight,
To tell abroad thy praises, thy miracles, thy might.
Still pilgrim feet are treading, along the holy way,
Hostess of England's Nazareth, receive us home today.

Hail Mary, ever blessed, the wells of water pure,
Which mark thy holy places, are signs that God doth cure.
For sick of soul and body, e'en since Richeldis' day,
They spring in benediction, beside the Pilgrim's Way.

Hail Mary, ever blessed, thy Name is great indeed,
For Jesus Christ our Saviour, was in thy womb conceiv'd.
Thy Name be ever praiséd increasing in this place,
And loud the Angel's greeting, 'Hail Mary, full of grace.'

Anon; music from the Württemberg Gesanbuch (1784)

TRANSLATIONS OF LITURGICAL HYMNS

LET ALL MORTAL FLESH KEEP SILENCE
Key: D minor; starting note: D

Let all mortal flesh keep silence,
And with fear and trembling stand;
Ponder nothing earthly minded,
For with blessing in his hand,
Christ our God to earth descendeth,
Our full homage to demand.

King of Kings yet born of Mary,
As of old on earth he stood,
Lord of Lords in human vesture,
In the Body and the Blood;
He will give to all the faithful
His own self for heavenly food.

Rank on rank the host of heaven
Spreads its vanguard on the way,
As the Light of light descendeth
From the realms of endless day,
That the powers of hell may vanish
As the darkness clears away.

At his feet the six-winged seraph;
Cherubim with sleepless eye,
Veil their faces to the Presence,
As with ceaseless voice they cry,
Alleluia! Alleluia!
Alleluia! Lord Most High.

Gerard Moultrie, 1864,
from the Liturgy of St James

197

COME, HOLY GHOST, CREATOR, COME

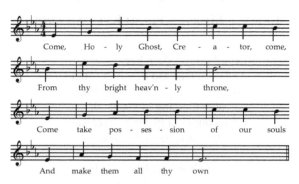

Come, Holy Ghost, Creator, come,
From thy bright heav'nly throne,
Come take possession of our souls
And make them all thy own

Thou who art called the Paraclete,
Best gift of God above,
The living spring, the living fire,
Sweet unction and true love.

Thou who art sevenfold in thy grace,
Finger of God's right hand
His promise teaching little ones
To speak and understand.

O guide our minds with thy blessed light,
With love our hearts inflame;
And with thy strength, which never decays
Confirm our mortal frame.

Far from us drive our deadly foe;
True peace unto us bring;
And through all perils lead us safe
Beneath thy sacred wing.

Through thee may we the Father know,
Through thee the eternal Son,
And thee, the Spirit of them both,
Thrice-blessèd Three in One.

All glory to the Father be,
With his co-equal Son;
The same to thee, great Paraclete,
While endless ages run.

A - men.

Veni creator Spiritus (see p152), *trans. anon, 1876*

SWEET SACRAMENT WE THEE ADORE

Jesus, my Lord, my God, my all,—

How can I love Thess as I ought?

And how re - vere— this won - d'rous gift,—

So far sur - pas - sing hope or thought.

Sweet Sa - cra - ment, we Thee a - dore.

O make us love Thee more— and more!

O make us love Thee more and more!

Had I but Mary's sinless heart,
To love thee with, my dearest King;
O with what bursts of fervent praise,
Thy goodness, Jesus, would I sing!

O, see, within a creature's hand,
The vast Creator deigns to be,
Reposing infant-like, as though
On Joseph's arm, on Mary's knee.

Thy body, soul, and Godhead, all--
O mystery of love divine!
I cannot compass all I have,
For all thou hast and art are mine.

Sound, sound his praises higher still,
And come ye Angels to our aid;
'Tis God, 'tis God, the very God,
Whose power both man and angels made.

Trans Fr Faber

199

GODHEAD HERE IN HIDING

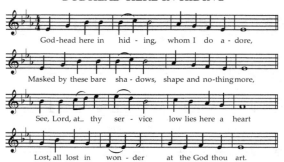

God-head here in hid - ing, whom I do a - dore,

Masked by these bare sha - dows, shape and no-thing more,

See, Lord, at thy ser - vice low lies here a heart

Lost, all lost in won - der at the God thou art.

Seeing, touching, tasting are in thee deceived:
How says trusty hearing? that shall be believed;
What God's Son has told me, take for truth I do;
Truth himself speaks truly or there's nothing true.

On the cross thy godhead made no sign to men,
Here thy very manhood steals from human ken:
Both are my confession, both are my belief,
And I pray the prayer of the dying thief.

I am not like Thomas, wounds I cannot see,
But can plainly call thee Lord and God as he;
Let me to a deeper faith daily nearer move,
Daily make me harder hope and dearer love.

O thou our reminder of Christ crucified,
Living Bread, the life of us for whom he died,
Lend this life to me then: feed and feast my mind,
There be thou the sweetness man was meant to find.

Bring the tender tale true of the Pelican;
Bathe me, Jesu Lord, in what thy bosom ran—
Blood whereof a single drop has power to win
All the world forgiveness of its world of sin.

Jesu, whom I look at shrouded here below,
I beseech thee send me what I thirst for so,
Some day to gaze on thee face to face in light
And be blest for ever with thy glory's sight.

A - men.

Aquinas, Adoro te,
trans Gerard Manley Hopkins, S.J.

Other English Hymns

JERUSALEM
Key: D major; starting note: D

And did those feet in ancient time,
Walk upon England's mountains green:
And was the holy Lamb of God,
On England's pleasant pastures seen!

And did the Countenance Divine,
Shine forth upon our clouded hills?
And was Jerusalem builded here,
Among these dark Satanic Mills?

Bring me my Bow of burning gold;
Bring me my Arrows of desire:
Bring me my Spear: O clouds unfold!
Bring me my Chariot of fire!

I will not cease from Mental Fight,
Nor shall my Sword sleep in my hand:
Till we have built Jerusalem,
In England's green & pleasant Land.

William Blake, 1808

OUR GOD OUR HELP IN AGES PAST

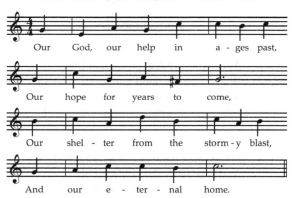

Our God, our help in a - ges past,

Our hope for years to come,

Our shel - ter from the storm - y blast,

And our e - ter - nal home.

Under the shadow of Thy throne
Thy saints have dwelt secure;
Sufficient is thine arm alone,
And our defense is sure.

Before the hills in order stood,
Or earth received her frame,
From everlasting thou art God,
To endless years the same.

Thy Word commands our flesh to dust,
'Return, ye sons of men:'
All nations rose from earth at first,
And turn to earth again.

A thousand ages in Thy sight
Are like an evening gone;
Short as the watch that ends the night
Before the rising sun.

The busy tribes of flesh and blood,
With all their lives and cares,

Are carried downwards by the flood,
And lost in following years.

Time, like an ever rolling stream,
Bears all its sons away;
They fly, forgotten, as a dream
Dies at the opening day.

Like flowery fields the nations stand
Pleased with the morning light;
The flowers beneath the mower's hand
Lie withering ere 'tis night.

Our God, our help in ages past,
Our hope for years to come,
Be thou our guard while troubles last,
And our eternal home.

Based on Ps. 89 (90); Isaac Watts, 1719

FOR ALL THE SAINTS
Key: G major; starting note: D

For all the saints, who from their labours rest,
Who thee by faith before the world confessed,
Thy Name, O Jesus, be forever blessed.
    Alleluia, Alleluia!

Thou wast their Rock, their Fortress and their Might;
Thou, Lord, their Captain in the well fought fight;
Thou, in the darkness drear, their one true Light.
    Alleluia, Alleluia!

For the apostles' glorious company,
Who bearing forth the cross o'er land and sea,
Shook all the mighty world, we sing to thee:
    Alleluia, Alleluia!

For the Evangelists, by whose blessed word,
Like fourfold streams, the garden of the Lord,
Is fair and fruitful, be thy Name adored.
   Alleluia, Alleluia!

For Martyrs, who with rapture kindled eye,
Saw the bright crown descending from the sky,
And seeing, grasped it, thee we glorify.
   Alleluia, Alleluia!

O may thy soldiers, faithful, true, and bold,
Fight as the saints who nobly fought of old,
And win, with them the victor's crown of gold.
   Alleluia, Alleluia!

O blest communion, fellowship divine!
We feebly struggle, they in glory shine;
All are one in thee, for all are thine.
   Alleluia, Alleluia!

And when the strife is fierce, the warfare long,
Steals on the ear the distant triumph song,
And hearts are brave, again, and arms are strong.
   Alleluia, Alleluia!

The golden evening brightens in the west;
Soon, soon to faithful warriors comes their rest;
Sweet is the calm of paradise the blessed.
   Alleluia, Alleluia!

But lo! there breaks a yet more glorious day;
The saints triumphant rise in bright array;
The King of glory passes on his way.
   Alleluia, Alleluia!

From earth's wide bounds, from ocean's farthest coast,
Through gates of pearl streams in the countless host,
Singing to Father, Son and Holy Ghost:
   Alleluia, Alleluia!

William Walsham How, 1864

BATTLE HYMN OF THE REPUBLIC
Key: B flat major; starting note: F

Mine eyes have seen the glory of the coming of the
    Lord:
He is trampling out the vintage where the grapes of
    wrath are stored;
He hath loosed the fateful lightning of his terrible
    swift sword:
His truth is marching on.

    Glory, glory, hallelujah! (x3)
    His truth is marching on.

I have seen him in the watch-fires of a hundred
    circling camps,
They have builded him an altar in the evening dews
    and damps;
I can read his righteous sentence by the dim and
    flaring lamps:
His day is marching on.

I have read a fiery gospel writ in burnished rows of
    steel:
"As ye deal with my contemners, so with you my
    grace shall deal;
Let the Hero, born of woman, crush the serpent with
    his heel,
His truth is marching on."

He has sounded forth the trumpet that shall never call
    retreat:
He is sifting out the hearts of men before his judgment
    -seat:
Oh, be swift, my soul, to answer him! be jubilant, my
    feet!
Our God is marching on.

In the beauty of the lilies Christ was born across the
    sea,
With a glory in his bosom that transfigures you and
    me:
As he died to make men holy, let us die to make men

free,
While God is marching on.

He is coming like the glory of the morning on the
        wave,
He is Wisdom to the mighty, he is Succour to the-
        brave,
So the world shall be his footstool, and the soul of
        Time his slave,
Our God is marching on.

Julia Ward Howe, 1861

I VOW TO THEE, MY COUNTRY
Tune: Thaxted; key: E flat major; starting note: D

I vow to thee, my country—all earthly things above—
Entire and whole and perfect, the service of my love;
The love that asks no question, the love that stands the
        test,
That lays upon the altar the dearest and the best;
The love that never falters, the love that pays the price,
The love that makes undaunted the final sacrifice.

I heard my country calling, away across the sea,
Across the waste of waters she calls and calls to me.
Her sword is girded at her side, her helmet on her
        head,
And round her feet are lying the dying and the dead.
I hear the noise of battle, the thunder of her guns,
I haste to thee my mother, a son among thy sons.

And there's another country, I've heard of long ago—
Most dear to them that love her, most great to them
        that know;
We may not count her armies, we may not see her
        King;
Her fortress is a faithful heart, her pride is suffering;
And soul by soul and silently her shining bounds
        increase,
And her ways are ways of gentleness, and all her paths
        are peace.

Cecil Spring-Rice, 1912 and 1918

ONWARD, CHRISTIAN SOLDIERS

On- ward, Christ-ian sol - diers, march-ing as to war,

with the cross of Je - sus go - ing on be - fore.

Christ, the roy - al Mast - er, leads a-gainst the foe;

for-ward in - to bat - tle__ see his ban-ners go!

On- ward, Christ-ian sol - diers, march-ing as to__ war,

with the cross of Je - sus go - ing on be - fore.

At the sign of triumph Satan's host doth flee;
on then, Christian soldiers, on to victory!
Hell's foundations quiver at the shout of praise;
brothers, lift your voices, loud your anthems raise.

Like a mighty army moves the church of God;
brothers, we are treading where the saints have trod.
We are not divided, all one body we,
one in hope and doctrine, one in charity.

Crowns and thrones may perish, kingdoms rise and wane,
but the church of Jesus constant will remain.
Gates of hell can never gainst that church prevail;
we have Christ's own promise, and that cannot fail.

Onward then, ye people, join our happy throng,
blend with ours your voices in the triumph song.
Glory, laud, and honour unto Christ the King,
this through countless ages men and angels sing.

Sabine Baring-Gould, 1865

207

ABIDE WITH ME

A - bide with me: fast falls the e - ven - tide;

The dark-ness deep - ens; Lord, with me a - bide:

When oth - er help - ers fail, and com-forts flee,

Help of the help-less, O a - bide with me.

Swift to its close ebbs out life's little day;
Earth's joys grow dim; its glories pass away;
Change and decay in all around I see;
O thou who changest not, abide with me.

I need thy presence every passing hour.
What but thy grace can foil the tempter's power?
Who, like thyself, my guide and stay can be?
Through cloud and sunshine, Lord, abide with me.

I fear no foe, with thee at hand to bless;
Ills have no weight, and tears no bitterness.
Where is death's sting? Where, grave, thy victory?
I triumph still, if thou abide with me.

Hold thou thy cross before my closing eyes;
Shine through the gloom and point me to the skies.
Heaven's morning breaks, and earth's vain shadows
    flee;
In life, in death, O Lord, abide with me.

Henry Francis Lyte, 1847

French Hymns from Chartres

CHARTRES SONNE

Chart - res son - ne, Chart - res t'ap - pel - le!

Gloi - re, hon - neur au Christ - Roi!

Je Vous a - do - re, mon Sei-gneur et mon Dieu,

Dieu de lu - miè - re, Di - vin Ma - jest - é,

Vos cré - a - tu - res chant - ent Vot - re Splen - dour.

Je Vous adore, mon Seigneur et mon Dieu, *(bis)*
Par la souffrance, sur l'arbre de la Croix, *(bis)*
Jésus, Vous êtes l'Instrument du Salut. *(bis)*

Je Vous adore, mon Seigneur et mon Dieu, *(bis)*
Sauveur du monde, Maître de l'univers, *(bis)*
Votre puissance soumettra les nations. *(bis)*

Je Vous adore, mon Seigneur et mon Dieu, *(bis)*
Dans la détresse, en Vous je me confie, *(bis)*
Je m'abandonne à Votre Volonté. *(bis)*

Je Vous adore, mon Seigneur et mon Dieu, *(bis)*
Vous mon refuge, soyez mon réconfort, *(bis)*
En Vous mon âme trouvera le repos. *(bis)*

Je Vous adore, mon Seigneur et mon Dieu, *(bis)*
Faites que j'aime tout ce que Vous aimez, *(bis)*

Et venez prendre possession de mon cœur. *(bis)*

O Notre Dame, ranimez notre Foi, *(bis)*
Dans les épreuves, gardez-nous l'espérance, *(bis)*
Vierge Marie, donnez-nous la Charité. *(bis)*

En Pèlerinage, Saint Louis guide nos pas, *(bis)*
Devant nos marches, déploie ton étendard, *(bis)*
Autour de Pierre, forme notr(e) unité. *(bis)*

O Sainte Georges, apprends-nous à prier, *(bis)*
Par ton exemple, sanctifie notr(e) ardeur, *(bis)*
Saint d'Angletere, sauve notre patrie. *(bis)*

Michel Archange, éclairez nos chemins, *(bis)*
Prince des anges, venez nous secourir, *(bis)*
De par le monde, terrassez le Malin. *(bis)*

Chez Nous (Chartres Hymn)

Chez nous, soy - ez Rei - ne, Nous som - mes à vous;

Ré - gnez en sou - ve - rai - ne Chez mous, chez nous.

Soy - ez la ma - do - ne Qu'on pri - e à ge - noux,

Qui sou - rit et par - don - ne Chez nous, chez nous.

L'Arch-ange qui s'in - cli - ne Vous lou - e au nom du ciel.

Don - nez la paix di - vi - ne A no - tre cœur mor - tel.

Vous êtes notre Mère,
Portez à votre Fils
La fervente prière
De vos enfants chéris.

Gardez, ô Vierge pure,
O Cœur doux entre tous
Nos âmes sans souillure,
Nos cœurs vaillants et doux.

Dites à ceux qui peinent
Et souffrent sans savoir
Combien lourde est la haine,
Combien doux est l'espoir.

Lorsque la nuit paisible
Nous invite au sommeil,
Près de nous, invisible,
Restez jusqu'au réveil.

Par vous que votre vie
Soit digne des élus,
Et notre âme ravie,
Au ciele, verra Jésus.

Soyez pour nous la Reine
De douce charité,
Et bannissez la haine
De toute la cité.

A notre heure dernière
Accueillez dans les cieux
A la maison du Père
Notre retour joyeux.

Secular English Songs

The National Anthem
Key: G major; starting note: G

God save our gracious Queen!
Long live our noble Queen!
God save the Queen!
Send her victorious,
Happy and glorious,
Long to reign over us:
God save The Queen!

O Lord our God arise,
Scatter her enemies,
And make them fall:
Confound their politics,
Frustrate their knavish tricks,
On thee our hopes we fix:
God save us all.

Thy choicest gifts in store,
On her be pleased to pour;
Long may she reign:
May she defend our laws,
And ever give us cause
To sing with heart and voice
God save the Queen!

God bless our native land,
May heaven's protective hand
Still guard our shore;
May peace her power extend,
Foe be transformed to friend,
And Britain's power depend
On war no more.

May just and righteous laws
Uphold the public cause,
And bless our isle.
Home of the brave and free,
Fair land and liberty,
We pray that still on thee
Kind heaven may smile.

Nor in this land alone
But be God's mercies known
From shore to shore!
Lord make the nations see,
That men should brothers be,
And form one family,
The wide world o'er.

John Bull, 1619, attrib.

AULD LANG SYNE
Key: F major; starting note: C

Should auld acquaintance be forgot,
and never brought to mind ?
Should auld acquaintance be forgot,
and auld lang syne?

*For auld lang syne, my jo, for auld lang syne,
we'll tak a cup o' kindness yet, for auld lang syne.*

And surely ye'll be your pint-stowp!
and surely I'll be mine!
And we'll tak a cup o' kindness yet,
for auld lang syne.

We twa hae run about the braes,
and pu'd the gowans fine;
But we've wander'd mony a weary fit,
sin auld lang syne.

We twa hae paidl'd i' the burn,
frae morning sun till dine;
But seas between us braid hae roar'd
sin auld lang syne.

And there's a hand, my trusty fiere!
and gie's a hand o' thine!
And we'll tak a right gude-willy waught,
for auld lang syne.

Robert Burns, 1788

RULE BRITANNIA

When Brit - ain first,_____ at Heav'n's com - mand,

A - rose_____ from out the a - zure main;

A - rose, a - rose, a - rose from out the a - zure main,

This was the char - ter, the char - ter of the land;

And guard - ian an - gels sang this strain:

"Rule, Bri - tan - nia! Bri - tan - nia! Rule the waves:

Bri - tons ne - ver ne - ver ne - ver shall be slaves."

The nations, not so blest as thee,
Must, in their turns, to tyrants fall;
Must in, must in, must in their turns, to tyrants fall;
While thou shalt flourish, shalt flourish great and
    free,
The dread and envy of them all.

Still more majestic shalt thou rise,
More dreadful, from each foreign stroke;
More dreadful, dreadful, dreadful, from each
    foreign stroke;

As the loud blast, the blast that tears the skies,
Serves but to root thy native oak.

Thee haughty tyrants ne'er shall tame:
All their attempts to bend thee down,
All their, all their, all their attempts to bend thee
    down,
Will but arouse, arouse thy generous flame;
But work their woe, and thy renown.

To thee belongs the rural reign;
Thy cities shall with commerce shine:
Thy cities, cities, cities shall with commerce shine:
All thine shall be, shall be the subject main,
And every shore it circles thine.

The Muses, still with freedom found,
Shall to thy happy coast repair;
Shall to, shall to, shall to thy happy coast repair;
Blest Isle! With matchless, with matchless beauty
    crown'd,
And manly hearts to guard the fair.

James Thomson, 1763;
music by Thomas Arne (1710–1778)

LOCH LOMOND

By yon bon-nie banks, and by yon bon-nie braes,

Where the sun shines bright on Loch Lo - mond,

Where me and my true love were ev-er want to gae,

On the bon-nie, bon-nie banks o' Loch Lo - mond.

Oh! ye'll tak' the high road and I'll tak' the low road,

And I'll be in Scot-land a-fore ye:

But me and my true love will ne-ver meet a-gin,

On the bon-nie, bon-nie banks o' Loch Lo - mond.

'Twas there that we parted, in yon shady glen,
On the steep, steep side o' Ben Lomond,
Where, in purple hue, the Hielan' hills we view,
And the moon comin' out in the gloamin'.

The wee birdies sing and the wild flowers spring,
And in sunshine the waters are sleepin';
But the broken heart it ken, nae second spring
    agin,
Tho' the waefu' may cease frae their greetin'.

Anon, 1841

216

Skye Boat Song

Chorus

Speed bon - nie boat, like a bird on the wing,

"On - wards!" the sail - ors cry. Car - ry the lad that's

born to be king, o - ver the sea to Skye.

Verse

Loud the winds howl, loud the waves roar,

thun - der-claps rend the air; baf - fled, our foes

stand on the shore. Fol - low they will not dare.

Though the waves leap, soft shall ye sleep,
Ocean's a royal bed;
Rocked in the deep, Flora will keep
Watch by your weary head.

Many's the lad fought on that day,
Well the claymore could wield;
When the night came, silently lay
Dead on Culloden's field.

Burned are our homes, exile and death
Scatter the loyal men;
Yet, e'er the sword cool in the sheath,
Charlie will come again.

Sir Harold Boulton, 1884

MEN OF HARLECH

Hark! I hear the foe ad-vanc-ing Bar-béd steeds are
Men of Har-lech, lie ye dream-ing? See ye not their

proud ly pranc-ing, Hel-mets in the sun-beams glanc-ing
fal chions gleam-ing, While their pen-nons gai-ly stream-ing

Glit-ter through the trees. From the rocks re-
Flut-ter in the breeze?

bound-ing, Let the war cry sound-ing

Sum-mon all at Cam-bria's call, The haught-y___ foe___ sur-

round-ing, Men of Har-lech, on to glo-ry!

See your ban-ner famed in stor-y Waves these burn-ing

words be-fore ye "Bri-tain scorns to yield!"

'Mid the fray, see dead and dying,
Friend and foe together lying;
All around, the arrows flying,
Scatter sudden death!
Frighten'd steeds are wildly neighing,
Brazen trumpets hoarsely braying,
Wounded men for mercy praying
With their parting breath!

See! They're in disorder!
Comrades, keep close order!
Ever they shall rue the day
They ventured o'er the border!
Now the Saxon flies before us!
Vict'ry's banner floateth o'er us!
Raise the loud exulting chorus
"Britain wins the field."

Thomas Oliphant, 1862

Part V:
The Walsingham
Pilgrimage

NOTES ON THE ROUTE

ELY

Ely is the home of **Saint Etheldreda,** a seventh century East Anglian princess, Fenland queen and Abbess of Ely. Saint Etheldreda was born circa 639 AD. She was married twice, but both times on the condition that she would remain a virgin. When her second husband attempted to claim full marital rights she retired to a convent.

She founded a double monastery at the site of Ely Cathedral and was confirmed its abbess. She died on 23 June 679 of a tumour on her neck. When her tomb was opened in in 695 her body, found incorrupt with the tumour healed, was enshrined in the Church. Her shrine in Ely Cathedral became one of the most popular places of pilgrimage until its destruction under Henry VIII.

At some time in the Middle Ages the Saint's left hand was detached and placed in its own reliquary. This was discovered in 1810 in a priest's hiding-hole in a Sussex farmhouse, so coming into the possession of the Duke of Norfolk, who gave it to his estate agent. In 1867 it passed to his grand-daughter, Sister Aquinas, a Dominican nun at Stone in Staffordshire.

The **Catholic Church of St Etheldreda** was built in 1891 opened in 1903. In 1953, as part of the celebrations of the Church's Jubilee Year the hand of Saint Etheldreda was moved here. It is now enshrined in a niche, behind a glass screen, over the font, adjacent to a statue of Saint Etheldreda.

Ely Cathedral

Although Saint Ethelreda established a monastery here in the seventh century, work on the current Cathedral began in the 11th century under the leadership of Abbot Simeon, and the monastic church became a cathedral in 1109. The monastery at Ely was dissolved by Henry VIII in 1539. Ely suffered less than many other monasteries, but even so, statues were destroyed together with carvings and stained glass and Saint Etheldreda's Shrine was destroyed.

The Cathedral was re-founded with a Chapter of eight canons in 1541 as was the Kings School. Robert Steward, the last Prior of the monastery, became the first Dean.

OXBURGH HALL

Oxburgh Hall was built by the Bedingfeld family in the 15th century and they have lived here ever since. Today most of the house belongs to the National Trust, but the Bedingfelds still live there and they still own the chapel. We are very grateful to Sir Henry and Lady (Mary) Bedingfeld for welcoming us to Oxburgh Hall and allowing us to use the chapel for Mass.

Although the chapel was built after the Catholic Relief Act (in 1836), the reredos is Medieval, and the chapel represents a continuation of the worship in more hidden places in the house itself during the times of persecution. Oxburgh is a very fine house, and boasts a priest hole.

Sir Henry Bendingfeld is a descendant of the Sir Henry Bedingfeld who was the custodian of Princess Elizabeth during the reign of Mary Tudor. Elizabeth is said to have remarked afterwards 'if we have anie prisoner whom we would have hardlie and strictly kept, we send him to you.' He refused to sign the Act of Uniformity, and the house became a centre for Catholic worship. Washing was hung out to dry on the hedges to signal that Mass was to be said. A later Sir Henry fought for the King in the Civil War and was imprisoned in the Tower of London for two years after his capture.

CASTLE ACRE PRIORY

The Priory at Castle Acre was founded in 1189; the community were Benedictines from Cluny, and later became independent. It was dissolved in 1537.

WALSINGHAM: THE MEDIEVAL SHRINE

In the medieval world, this place of pilgrimage ranked fourth after Jerusalem, Compostela and Rome, and it was the only one of the four to be dedicated specifically to the Blessed Virgin.

The Slipper Chapel was built in 1340 and dedicated to St

Catherine of Alexandria (who appears on the reredos today). Its name derives from 'slipe' or 'slype', a reference to the passage ('slyping') of pilgrims on their way to Walsingham. It marks the start of the 'Holy Mile', the last mile of pilgrimage to the Holy House in Walsingham.

Walsingham Priory

The Priory was a community of Augustinian Canons Regular, founded in 1153. In 1537 the Sub-Prior and eleven others were hanged, drawn and quartered on the charge of fomenting opposition to the dissolution of the lesser monasteries. In 1538 the Priory, and the shrine it housed, was surrendered to the King, and the site was sold for secular uses (a Manor House was later built there). The shrine image was taken to London and, with many other holy images, burnt at Chelsea.

The Priory's eastern gable survives, some 70 feet high, flanked by staircases and turrets. The spot where England's little House of Nazareth once stood, the shrine of Our Lady of Walsingham, is marked in the grass.

Origins of pilgrimages to Walsingham

During the reign of Edward the Confessor, only five years before the Norman invasion of 1066, 'the Lady Richeldis', the lady of the manor of Walsingham, had a dream in which the Blessed Virgin transported her to the Holy House of Nazareth. Our Lady requested that one of its like should be built in Walsingham. The dream was repeated three times, and Richeldis did her best to carry out Our Lady's wish.

Richeldis' builders, however, were unable to complete the task, and overnight she saw that the house had been built by angels, not in the place she had chosen, but some two hundred feet away. In this place, Mary had explained, the people would celebrate the Annunciation, 'the root of man's gracious redemption'. She also delivered a promise to future generations who might visit Walsingham: 'Whosoever seeks my help here will not go away empty-handed'. The little shrine was to become a place of prayer and consolation for people from all corners of the world.

According to the Domesday Book, the Manor of Walsingham belonged, before the Conquest, to King Harold
II; the Lady of the Manor would therefore have been his
queen, Edith the Fair, niece of King Edward and grand-
daughter of King Ethelred. 'Richeldis' means 'rich and
fair', a title appropriate to Edith. Though always recog-
nised as a royal foundation, the connection with the English royal house was not something the Norman kings
wished to emphasise.

After her husband's defeat and death at Hastings, Edith
fled to the protection of her Danish relations. Her daughter Gytha married Vladimir II Monomakh, Grand Prince
of Kiev.

THE CATHOLIC SHRINE TODAY

In 1896 the Slipper Chapel was purchased by a local
convert, Miss Charlotte Pearson Boyd, and donated to
Downside Abbey to be restored to Catholic worship.

In 1897 Pope Leo XIII blessed a new statue 'for the restored ancient sanctuary of Our Lady of Walsingham'.
This was sent from Rome and placed in the Holy House
Chapel at the newly built Roman Catholic parish church
of King's Lynn (the village of Walsingham was within
the parish) and the first public post-Reformation pilgrimage took place to the Slipper Chapel at Walsingham that
year.

The Slipper Chapel became the location of the Catholic
Shrine in 1934. The 'Reconciliation Chapel' was com-
pleted in 1982. The Shrine was raised to the status of
Minor Basilica by Pope Francis in 2015.

The statue of Our Lady in the Slipper Chapel today is
based on the fifteenth century seal of Walsingham Priory,
which shows the original shrine image. Mary wears a
Saxon crown, a symbol of her ancient queenship, as she
reaches out in motherhood to all and presents her Son to
the world. Today's image was crowned by mandate of
Pope Pius XII in 1954 and blessed by Pope St John Paul
II in 1982.

Pilgrims' Blessings for the
Start of the Pilgrimage: Ely

IN viam pacis * et prosperitátis dírigat vos omnípotens et miséricors Dóminus: et Angelus Rápha-el comitétur vobíscum in via, ut cum pace, salúte et gáudio revertámini ad própria.

Benedíctus Dóminus, Deus Isra-ël * quia visitávit, et fecit redemptiónem plebis su-æ.

Et eréxit cornu sa*lú*tis **nobis** * in domo David *pú*eri **sui.**
Sicut locútus est per *os* sanc**tó**rum,
　　* qui a sǽculo sunt, prophe*tá*rum **e**ius:
Salútem ex ini*mí*cis **nos**tris,
　　* et de manu ómnium *qui* o**dé**runt nos:
Ad faciéndam misericórdiam cum *pá*tribus **nos**tris:
　　* et memorári testaménti *sui* **sanc**ti:
Iusiurándum, quod iurávit ad Abraham *pat*rem **nos**trum,
　　* da*tú*rum se **no**bis;
Ut sine timóre, de manu inimicórum nostrórum *li*ber**á**ti,
　　* serviámus **il**li.
In sanctitáte et iustítia *co*ram **ip**so,
　　* ómnibus di*é*bus **nos**tris.
Et tu puer, prophéta Altíss*imi* vo**cá**beris: * præíbis enim
　　ante fáciem Dómini paráre *vi*as **e**ius:

Ad dandam sciéntiam salútis *ple*bi **e**ius:
　　* in remissiónem pecca*tó*rum e**ó**rum:
Per víscera misericórdiæ *Dei* **nos**tri:

Pilgrims' Blessings for the Start of the Pilgrimage: Ely

Antiphon: In the way of peace and prosperity may the almighty and merciful Lord lead you; and may the angel Raphael be your companion on the journey, so that in peace, health and happiness you may return unto your own.

Canticle of Zachary.

Blessed be the Lord God of Israel: because he hath visited and wrought the redemption of his people;

And hath raised up an horn of salvation to us, in the house of David his servant.
As he spoke by the mouth of his holy prophets, who are from the beginning:
Salvation from our enemies and from the hand of all that hate us;
To perform mercy to our fathers and to remember his holy testament.
The oath, which he swore to Abraham our father, that he would grant to us;
That, being delivered from the hand of our enemies, we may serve him without fear,
In holiness and justice before him, all our days.

And thou, child, shalt be called the prophet of the Highest; for thou shalt, go before the face of the Lord to prepare his ways:
To give knowledge of salvation to his people, unto the remission of their sins;
Through the bowels of the mercy of our God, in which

       * in quibus visitávit nos, óriens ex alto:
Illumináre his qui in ténebris et in umbra mortis sedent:
       * ad dirigéndos pedes nostros in viam pacis.
Glória Patri et Fílio, * et Spirítui Sancto.
Sicut erat in princípio, et nunc, et semper, * et in sæcula
sæculórum. Amen.

Antiphon

Kýrie, eléison. Christe, eléison. Kýrie, eléison.
Pater noster *secreto usque ad*
℣. Et ne nos indúcas in tentatiónem.
℟. Sed líbera nos a malo.
℣. Salvos fac servos tuos.
℟. Deus meus, sperántes in te.
℣. Mitte nobis, Dómine, auxílium de sancto.
℟. Et de Sion tuére nos.
℣. Esto nobis, Dómine, turris fortitúdinis.
℟. A fácie inimíci.
℣. Nihil proficiat inimícus in nobis.
℟. Et fílius iniquitátis non appónat nocére nobis.
℣. Benedíctus Dóminus die cotídie.
℟. Próperum iter fáciat nobis Deus salutárium nostrórum.

℣. Vias tuas, Dómine, demónstra nobis.
℟. Et sémitas tuas édoce nos.
℣. Utinam dirigántur viæ nostræ.
℟. Ad custodiéndas justificatiónes tuas.
℣. Erunt prava in dirécta.
℟. Et áspera in vias planas.
℣. Angelis suís Deus mandávit de te.
℟. Ut custódiant te in ómnibus viis tuis.
℣. Dómine, exáudi oratiónem meam.
℟. Et clamor meus ad te véniat.
℣. Dóminus vobíscum.
℟. Et cum spíritu tuo.

    Orémus.
Deus, qui fílios Israel per maris médium sicco vestígio ire
fecísti, quique tribus Magis iter ad te stella duce pandísti:
tríbue nobis, quǽsumus, iter prósperum, tempúsque
tranquíllum; ut, Angelo tuo sancto cómite, ad eum, quo

the Orient from on high hath visited us;

To enlighten them that sit in darkness and in the shadow of death; to direct our feet into the way of peace.

Glory be to the Father, and to the Son, and to the Holy Ghost.

As it was in the beginning, is now, and ever shall be. Amen.

Antiphon

Lord, have mercy on us. Christ, have mercy on us. Lord, have mercy on us.

Our Father *inaudibly until*

℣. And lead us not into temptation.

℟. But deliver us from evil.

℣. Save thy servants.

℟. O my God, that trust in thee.

℣. Send us, O Lord, help from the sanctuary.

℟. And defend us out of Sion.

℣. Be unto us, O Lord, a tower of strength,

℟. Against the face of the enemy.

℣. Let the enemy have no advantage over us,

℟. Nor the son of iniquity have power to hurt us.

℣. Blessed be the Lord day by day,

℟. May the God of our salvation make our journey prosperous to us.

℣. Show, O Lord, thy ways to us,

℟. And teach us thy paths.

℣. O that our ways may be directed,

℟. To keep thy justifications.

℣. The crooked shall become straight,

℟. And the rough ways plain

℣. God hath given his angels charge over you,

℟. To keep you in all your ways.

℣. O Lord, hear my prayer,

℟. And let my cry come unto thee.

℣. The Lord be with you.

℟. And with thy spirit.

Let us pray.

O God, who didst lead the sons of Israel dry-shod through the sea, and didst show the way to the three Magi by the guidance of a star; we beseech thee to grant us pilgrims a happy journey and a peaceful time, that accompanied by

pérgimus, locum, ac demum ad ætérnæ salútis portum felíciter valeámus perveníre.

Deus, qui Abraham púerum tuum de Ur Chaldæórum edúctum, per omnes suæ peregrinatiónis vias illǽsum custodísti: quǽsumus, ut nos fámulos tuos custodíre dignéris; esto nobis, Dómine, in procínctu suffrágium, in via solácium, in æstu umbráculum, in plúvia et frígore teguméntum, in lassitúdine vehículum, in adversitáte præsídium, in lúbrico báculus, in naufrágio portus: ut te duce, quo téndimus, próspere perveniámus, et demum incólumes ad própria revertámur.

Adésto, quǽsumus, Dómine, supplicatiónibus nostris: et viam famulórum tuórum in salútis tuæ prosperitáte dispóne; ut inter omnes viæ et vitæ hujus varietátes tuo semper protegántur auxílio.

Præsta, quǽsumus, omnípotens Deus: ut família tua per viam salútis incédat; et, beáti Ioánnis Præcursóris hortaménta sectándo, ad eum, quem prædíxit, secúra pervéniat, Dóminum nostrum Iesum Christum, Fílium tuum.

Exáudi, Dómine, preces nostras, et iter famulórum tuórum propítius comitáre, atque misericórdiam tuam, sicut ubíque es, ita ubíque largíre: quátenus a cunctis adversitátibus tua opitulatióne defénsi, gratiárum tibi réferant actiónem. Per Christum Dóminum nostrum.

℟. Amen.

Pax et benedíctio Dei omnipoténtis, Patris, et Fílii, ✠ et Spíritus Sancti, descéndat super vos, et máneat semper.

℟. Amen.

Et aspergantur aqua benedicta.

thy holy angel we may be able safely to reach our present destination, and to come finally to the haven of eternal salvation.

O God, who didst lead thy servant, Abraham out of Ur of the Chaldeans, safeguarding him in all his wanderings—guide us thy servants, we implore thee. Be unto us support in the enterprise, relief on the journey, shade in the heat, shelter in the rain and cold, a conveyance in tiredness, protection in adversity, a staff in insecurity, and a haven in shipwreck; so that under thy guidance we may successfully reach our destination, and finally return safe to our homes.

Give heed, we pray thee, Lord to our entreaties: and order the path of thy servants in what is agreeable to thy salvation, that in all the uncertainties of this journey and life, we may ever be defended by thy protecting help.

Grant, we beseech thee, almighty God, that we thy servants may advance by a safe route; and that, by heeding the exhortations of Blessed John the Precursor, we may come safely to him whom John foretold, our Lord Jesus Christ, thy Son.

Graciously hear, O Lord, our prayers, and in thy mercy accompany the journey of thy servants; and just as thou art everywhere present, so too dispense thy mercy in every place; that protected by thy help from all misfortunes, we may render thanksgiving unto thee. Through Christ our Lord.

℟. Amen.

May the peace and blessing of almighty God, Father, Son, ✠ and Holy Spirit come upon you and remain with you for all time.

℟. Amen.

They are sprinkled with holy water.

DE PROFUNDIS, AT CASTLE ACRE PRIORY

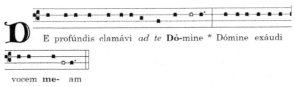

D
E profúndis clamávi *ad te* **Dó**-mine * Dómine exáudi
vocem **me**- am

Fíant áures túæ *inten*den**tes**: * in vócem deprecatiónis
méæ.

Si iniquitátes observáveris, **Dó**mine: * Dómine, quis susti-
nébit?

Quia apud te propitiá*tio* est: * et propter légem túam sustínui te, **Do**mine.

Sustínuit ánima méa in *verbo* **é**ius: * sperávit ánima méa
in **Dó**mino.

A custódia matutína us*que ad* **nó**ctem: * spéret Israël in
Dómino.

Quia apud Dóminum mi*seri*cór**dia**: * et copiósa apud éum
re**dém**ptio.

Et ípse ré*dimet* **Is**ræl: * ex ómnibus iniquitátibus **e**ius.

Requiem ætérnam * dona eis, **Do**mine.

Et *lux per*pé**tua** * lúceat **é**is.

℣. Requiescant in pace.

℟. Amen.

℣. Domine, exaudi orationem meam,

℟. Et clamor meus ad te veniat.

Oremus.
Fidelium Deus omnium conditor et redemptor, animabus
famulorum famularumque tuarum remissionem cuncto-
rum tribue peccatorum: ut iudulgentiam, quam semper
optaverunt, piis supplicationibus consequantur. Qui vivis
et regnas in sæcula sæculorum.

℟. Amen.

℣. Requiem ætérnam dona eis, Domine.

℟. Et lux perpetua luceat eis.

℣. Requiescant in pace.

℟. Amen.

DE PROFUNDIS, AT CASTLE ACRE PRIORY

[Ps. 129]

Out of the depths I have cried unto thee, O Lord, Lord, hear my voice.

Let thine ears be attentive: to the voice of my supplication.

If thou, O Lord, shalt observe iniquities: Lord, who can shall endure it?

For with thee there is merciful forgiveness: and by reason of thy law I have waited for thee, O Lord.

My soul hath relied on his word: my soul hath hoped in the Lord.

From the morning watch even unto night: let Israel hope in the Lord.

Because with the Lord there is mercy: and with him plentiful redemption.

And he shall redeem Israel: from all his iniquities.

Eternal rest give unto them, O Lord.

And let perpetual light shine upon them.

℣. May they rest in peace.

℟. Amen.

℣. Lord, hear my prayer.

℟. And let my cry come unto thee.

Let us pray.

O God, the Creator and Redeemer of all the faithful; grant to the souls of thy servants departed the remission of all their sins, that by our pious supplication they may obtain that pardon which they have always desired. Who livest and reignest world without end.

℟. Amen.

℣. Eternal rest give unto them, O Lord.

℟. And let perpetual light shine upon them.

℣. May they rest in peace.

℟. Amen.

GLORIA LAUS, ON ENTERING
THE CATHOLIC SHRINE

Gló-ri- a, laus et honor, ti-bi sit, Rex Christe Redémptor: Cu-i pu-e- rí-le de-cus prompsit Hosánna pi- um.

1. Isra- ël es tu Rex, Daví-dis et íncli-ta pro-les: Nómine
qui in Dómi-ni, Rex bene-dí-cte, venis. Glória, Laus.

2. Cœtus in excél-sis te laudat cǽ- li-cus omnis, Et mortá-
lis homo, et cuncta cre-á- ta simul. Glória, Laus.

3. Plebs Hebrǽ-a ti-bi cum palmis óbvi- a venit: Cum pre-
ce, vo-to, hymnis, ádsumus ecce ti-bi. Glória, Laus.

4. Hi ti-bi passú- ro solvé-bant mú-ni- a laudis: Nos ti-bi
regnánti pángimus ecce me-los. Glória, Laus.

5. Hi placu- é-re ti- bi, plá-ce- at devó- ti- o nostra: Rex bone, Rex clemens, cui bona cuncta placent. Glória, Laus.

Prayer at the Feet of Our Lady of Walsingham

O Mary, O glorious Mother of my Saviour, behold me at my journey's end kneeling within this venerable sanctuary where, through the centuries, thou hast been the object of the devotion and confidence of the faithful. In this place where thy name is so great, thy protection so assured, where thou hast showered so many notable favours on those who have sought thy intercession, I humbly claim a share in thy prayers. O Mary, our Lady of Walsingham, I have undertaken this journey, in order that I may obtain from thy Divine Son, Our Lord Jesus Christ, through thy powerful intercession, the conversion of England.

Pray, dear Mother, that our Lord may make good all that is imperfect in my requests and obtain for me the crowning of a heart completely surrendered to his Will. Amen

O Lord, Word Incarnate, Jesus of Nazareth, have mercy upon us. (*Say three times*) May the Divine Assistance remain always with us and may the souls of the faithful departed rest in peace. Amen.

Prayer to the Holy Ghost

Composed by Désiré-Joseph, Cardinal Mercier (d.1926) on a pilgrimage to Walsingham.

O Holy Spirit, soul of my soul, I adore thee. Enlighten, guide, strengthen and console me. Tell me what I ought to do and command me to do it. I promise to be submissive in all that thou shalt ask of me, and to accept all that thou permittest to happen to me: only show me thy will. Amen.

Mass follows in the Reconciliation Chapel, (see Propers on p60), followed by a Procession to the site of the Holy House, in the grounds of the ruined Priory. During the procession the Rosary is sung.

Te Deum, at Walsingham Priory

III.

T E De-um laudá-mus: * te Dóminum confi-témur. Te æ-

térnum Patrem omnis terra vene-rá-tur. Tibi omnes Angeli,

tibi cæli et univérsæ Potestá-tes: Tibi Cherubim et Séraphim

incessá-bi-li voce proclámant: Sanctus: Sanctus: Sanctus Dó-

minus De-us Sába-oth. Pleni sunt cæli et terra ma-iestátis gló-

ri-æ tu-æ. Te glo-ri-ó-sus Aposto-lórum chorus: Te Prophe-tá-

rum laudábi-lis númerus: Te Mártyrum candi-dátus laudat ex-

ércitus. Te per orbem terrárum sancta confi-té-tur Ecclési-a.

Patrem imménsæ ma-iestá-tis: Venerándum tu-um verum et

úni-cum Fí-li-um: Sanctum quoque Parácli-tum Spíri-tum. Tu

Rex gló-ri-æ, Christe. Tu Patris sempitérnus es Fí-li-us. Tu

ad li-berándum susceptúrus hóminem, non horru-ísti Vírginis

ú-terum. Tu devícto mortis acúle-o, aperu-ísti credéntibus reg-

na cæló-rum. Tu ad déxteram De-i sedes, in gló-ri-a Patris

Iudex créderis esse ventúrus. Te ergo quǽsumus, tu-is fámulis

súbveni, quos pre-ti-óso sánguine redemísti. Ætérna fac cum

Sanctis tu-is in gló-ri-a numerá- ri. Salvum fac pópulum tu-um

Dómine, et bénedic here-ditá-ti tu- æ. Et re-ge e-os, et ex-

tól-le illos usque in ætér-num. Per síngulos di-es, bene-dí-ci-

mus te. Et laudámus nomen tu-um in sǽculum, et in sǽculum

sǽcu-li. Dignáre Dómine di- e isto sine peccáto nos custodí-

re. Miseré-re nostri Dómine, mise-rére nostri. Fí-at mise-ricór-

di-a tu-a Dómine super nos, quemádmodum sperávimus in te.

In te Dómi-ne sperá- vi : non confúndar in æ-tér- num.

During the veneration of the Image, the following are sung: **The Litany of Our Lady** (p137) **Faith of Our Fathers** (p168)

Blessing of Pilgrims at Walsingham Priory

℣. Adiutórium nostrum in nómine Dómini.
℟. Qui fecit cælum et terram.

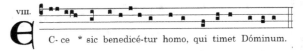

C- ce * sic benedicé-tur homo, qui timet Dóminum.

Psalmus 127

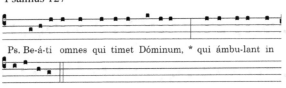

Ps. Be-á-ti omnes qui timet Dóminum, * qui ámbu-lant in vi- is e-ius.

Labóres mánuum tuárum quia manducábis:
    * beátus es, et bene *tí*bi **erit**.
Uxor tua sicut vitis ab*ún*dans, * in latéribus *do*mus **tuæ**.

Fílii tui sicut novéllæ oliv*árum*, * in circúitu *mensæ* **tuæ**.
Ecce sic benedicétur *ho*mo, * qui *ti*met **Dóminum**.
Benedícat tibi Dóminus ex *Sí*on:
    * et vídeas bona Ierúsalem ómnibus diébus *vitæ* **tuæ**.
Et vídeas fílios filiórum tu*órum*, * pacem *super* **Isra**el.

Glória Patri et *Fí*lio, * et Spir*í*tui **Sanc**to.

Sicut erat in princípio, et nunc, et *sem*per,
    * et in sǽcula sæcu*ló*rum. **A**men.

Antiphon

When the Veneration of the Image is complete the Chaplain blesses the pilgrims.

BLESSING OF PILGRIMS AT WALSINGHAM PRIORY

℣. Our help is in the name of the Lord.
℟. Who made heaven and earth

Antiphon:
Behold, thus shall he be blessed who feareth the Lord.

Psalm 127

Blessed are all that fear the Lord, that walk in His ways.

For thou shalt eat the labour of thy hands; happy art thou, and all shall be well with thee.
Thy wife shall be like the fruitful vine on the walls of thy dwelling;
Thy children like young olive plants round about thy table.
Behold, thus shall he be blessed who feareth the Lord.
May the Lord bless thee from Sion, and mayest thou see the prosperity of Jerusalem all the days of thy life.
And mayest thou see thy children's children. Peace be unto Israel!
Glory be to the Father, and to the Son, and to the Holy Ghost.
As it was in the beginning, is now, and ever shall be. Amen.

Antiphon

Kýrie, eléison. Christe, eléison. Kýrie, eléison.

Pater noster *secreto usque ad*
℣. Et ne nos indúcas in tentatiónem.
℞. Sed líbera nos a malo.
℣. Benedícti, qui véniunt in nómine Dómini.
℞. Benedícti vos a Dómino, qui fecit cælum et terram.

℣. Réspice, Dómine, in servos tuos, et in ópera tua.
℞. Et dírige eos in viam mandatórum tuórum.
℣. Dómine, exáudi oratiónem meam.
℞. Et clamor meus ad te véniat.
℣. Dóminus vobíscum.
℞. Et cum spíritu tuo.

Orémus.

Largíre, quæsumus, Dómine, fámulis tuis indulgéntiam placátus et pacem: ut páriter ab ómnibus mundéntur offensis, et secúra tibi mente desérviant.

Omnípotens sempitérne Deus, nostrórum témporum, vitǽque dispósitor, fámulis tuis contínuæ tranquillitátis largíre subsídium: ut, quos incólumes própriis labóribus reddísti, tua fácias protectióne secúros.

Deus, humílium visitátor, qui nos fratérna dilectióne consoláris: præténde societáti nostræ grátiam tuam; ut per eos, in quibus hábitas, tuum in nobis sentiámus advéntum. Per Dóminum.
℞. Amen.

Pax et benedíctio Dei omnipoténtis Patris, et Fílii, et ✠ Spíritus Sancti, descéndat super vos, et máneat semper.
℞. Amen.

Et aspergantur aqua benedicta.

Lord, have mercy on us. Christ, have mercy on us.
Lord, have mercy on us.
Our Father *inaudibly until*
℣. And lead us not into temptation.
℟. But deliver us from evil.
℣. Blessed are they that come in the name of the Lord.
℟. Blessed be you by the Lord, Who made heaven and
     earth.
℣. Regard, O Lord, thy servants and thy works.
℟. And direct them in observing thy precepts.
℣. O Lord, hear my prayer.
℟. And let my cry come unto thee.
℣. The Lord be with you.
℟. And with thy spirit.

Let us pray.

We beseech thee, Lord, be appeased, and lavish pardon
on thy faithful, and peace; that they may be cleansed
from all their sins, and may serve thee with tranquil
hearts.
     Almighty, everlasting God, Who dost dispose of
our life and our destinies, grant to thy faithful people
continued peace in abundance, that they whom thou dost
return to their former labors may bask in the security of
thy protection.
     O God, the Support of the lowly, Who dost
hearten us by thy brotherly love, bestow thy grace upon
our brotherhood, that by thy indwelling we may experience thy coming. Through our Lord, Jesus Christ.
℟. Amen.

May the blessing of almighty God, Father, Son, ✠ and
Holy Spirit come upon you and remain with you forever.
℟. Amen.

They are sprinkled with holy water.

Ant. 1.

Sal- ve, * Re-gí- na, mater mi-se-ricórdi- ae: Vi-ta dulcé- do, et spes nóstra, sal-ve. Ad te clamá-mus, éxsu-les fí-li- i Hevae. Ad te suspi-rá- mus, geméntes et flentes In hac lacrimá-rum valle. E- ia ergo, Advo-cá- ta nostra, illos tu- os mi-se-ri-córdes ócu-los ad nos convér- te. Et Iesum, benedí-ctum fructum ventris tu- i, no-bis post hoc exsí-li- um os-ténde. O cle-mens: O pi- a: O dulcis * Virgo Ma-rí- a.

SIMPLIFIED MAP OF
ELY

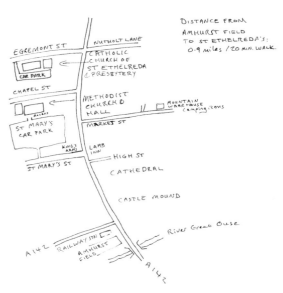

DISTANCE FROM
AMHURST FIELD
TO ST ETHELREDA's:
0.9 miles / 20 min. WALK.

The Walsingham Pilgrimage

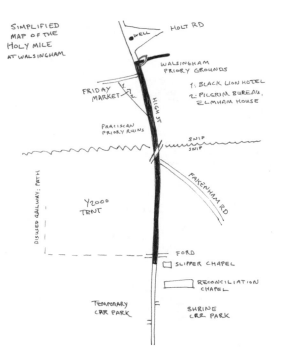

SIMPLIFIED MAP OF THE HOLY MILE AT WALSINGHAM

WELL

HOLT RD

WALSINGHAM PRIORY GROUNDS

1. BLACK LION HOTEL
2. PILGRIM BUREAU, ELMHAM HOUSE

FRIDAY MARKET

HIGH ST

FRANCISCAN PRIORY RUINS

SNIP SNIP

FAKENHAM RD

DISUSED RAILWAY: PATH

Y2000 TENT

FORD

SLIPPER CHAPEL

RECONCILIATION CHAPEL

TEMPORARY CAR PARK

SHRINE CAR PARK

PART VI:
OTHER
LATIN MASS SOCIETY
PILGRIMAGES

PILGRIMAGE TO HOLYWELL

St Winefride (from the *Catholic Encyclopedia*)

Born at Holywell, Wales, about 600; died at Gwytherin, Wales, 3 Nov., 660. Her father was Thevit, a Cambrian magnate, the possessor of three manors in what is now Flintshire; her mother Wenlo, a sister of St. Beuno and a member of a family closely connected with the kings of South Wales. ...St. Beuno ... built a chapel in which he said Mass and preached to the people. Winefride was then one of his most attentive listeners. Though only fifteen years old she gave herself to a life of devotion and austerity, passing whole nights watching in the church. Prior to the conquest of Wales the saint was known as Guenevra; after that her name was changed to the English form of Winefride. ...

The fame of her beauty and accomplishments had reached the ears of Caradoc, son of the neighbouring Prince Alen, who resolved to seek her hand in marriage. Coming in person to press his suit he entered the house of Thevit, and found Winefride alone, her parents having gone early to Mass. The knowledge that Winefride had resolved to quit the world and consecrate herself to God seemed only to add fuel to his passion, and he pleaded his cause with extraordinary vehemence, even proceeding to threats as he saw her turn indignantly away. At length, terrified at his words and alarmed for her innocence, the maiden escaped from the house, and hurried towards the church, where her parents were hearing Mass, that was being celebrated by her uncle, St. Beuno. Maddened by a disappointed passion, Caradoc pursued her and, overtaking her on the slope above the site of the present well, he drew his sword and at one blow severed her head from the body. The head rolled down the incline and, where it rested, there gushed forth a spring. St. Beuno, hearing of the tragedy, left the altar, and accompanied by the parents came to the spot where the head lay beside the spring. Taking up the maiden's head he carried it to where the body lay, covered both with his cloak, and then re-entered the church to finish the Holy Sacrifice. When Mass was ended he knelt beside the saint's body, offered up a fervent prayer to God, and ordered the cloak which covered it to be removed. Thereupon Winefride, as if awakening from a deep slumber, rose up with no sign of the severance of the head except a thin white circle round her neck. Seeing the murderer leaning on his sword with an insolent and defiant air, St. Beuno invoked the chastisement of heaven, and Caradoc fell dead on the spot, the popular belief being that the ground opened and swallowed him.

Miraculously restored to life, Winefride seems to have lived in almost perpetual ecstasy and to have had familiar converse with God. In fulfillment of her promise, she solemnly vowed virginity and poverty as a recluse. A convent was built on her father's land, where she became the abbess of a community of young maidens, and a chapel was erected over the well. St. Beuno left Holywell, and returned to Cærnarvon. Before he left the tradition is that he seated himself upon the stone, which now stands in the outer well pool, and there promised in the name of God "that whosoever on that spot should thrice ask for a benefit from God in the name of St. Winefride would obtain the grace he asked if it was for the good of his soul." ...After eight years spent at Holywell (reckoning from the departure of St. Beuno), St. Winefride, hearing of his death, received an inspiration to leave the convent and retire inland. There was reason to fear that Holywell would soon be no longer safe from the Saxon. The Kingdom of Northumbria was pressing upon the boarders of North Wales; Anglesea and Chester were already in the hands of the Saxon. It was time for the British recluses to seek the safety of the mountains; accordingly St. Winefride went upon her pilgrimage to seek for a place of rest. Ultimately she arrived at Gwytherin near the source of the River Elwy. This is still a most retired spot, where Welsh alone is spoken.

247

Some ten miles further across the vale of the Conway rises the double peak of Snowdon. St. Winefride was welcomed at Gwytherin by St. Elwy (Elerius), who gives his name to the River Elwy, and by whom the first life of the saint was written. She brought her companion religious with her, and found there other nuns governed by an abbess. She seems to have lived at Gwytherin as an acknowledged saint on earth, first in humble obedience to the abbess, and, after the latter's death, as abbess herself until her own death. Her chief feast is observed on 3 Nov., the other feast held in midsummer being that of her martyrdom. Her death was foreshown to her in a vision by Christ Himself.

During her life she performed many miracles, and after her death, up to the present day, countless wonders and favours continue to be worked and obtained through her intercession.

Holywell (from the *Catholic Encyclopedia*)

<u>The miraculous well</u>
For more than a thousand years this well has attracted numerous pilgrims. Two documents of the twelfth century, preserved in the British Museum, and printed by the Bollandists, give us its history, with the earliest record of the miraculous cures effected by its waters. These ancient cures included cases of dropsy, paralysis, gout, melancholia, sciatica, cancer, alienation of mind, blood spitting, obstinate cough, chronic pain and fluxion of the bowels, also deliverance from evil spirits. The concourse of pilgrims to the well continued in the sixteenth century during the days of persecution, and Dr. Thomas Goldwell, Bishop of St. Asaph, who went into exile at the accession of Elizabeth, obtained from the sovereign pontiff the confirmation of certain indulgences granted by Martin V (1417-31) to pilgrims who visited the well. In the seventeenth century, in spite of the severe penal laws, pilgrims still resorted to the well, and the record has been kept of

many remarkable cures, one being that of [Blessed] Father [Edward] Oldcorne, S.J., the martyr, who was healed miraculously of a gangrene that had formed in the roof of his mouth.

Origin and history of the well

...In 1093 the church at Holywell and the sacred fountain were given by Adeliza, Countess of Chester, to the monastery of St. Werburgh in that city. In 1115 Richard, Earl of Chester, her son, went on a pilgrimage to St. Winefride's Well. In 1240 David, son of Llewellyn, Prince of Wales, granted the church and well with extensive possessions to the monks of Basingwerk Abbey, who held them until 1537, the year of the dissolution. King Richard III ordered the sum of ten marks to be paid annually from the treasury for the support of the chapel of St. Winefride, and the stipend of the priest, and a few years later, probably before 1495, the beautiful buildings now surrounding the Well were erected.

Description of the well

The buildings referred to are in the perpendicular style, and were erected over the spring partly through the munificence of Margaret, Countess of Richmond and Derby, the mother of King Henry VII; but the armorial bearings introduced into the sculpture show that several noble Welsh families, including those of Stanley, Pennant, and Lewis, had a share in the work. Though time has dealt somewhat harshly with the stonework, sufficient remains to show that it was originally a most beautiful structure, abounding in delicate tracery and other carved work. The spring forms a basin enclosed by an octagonal parapet, from which rise eight delicately chiselled columns; these meet overhead in a beautiful traceried canopy, forming a crypt or vault. Above this stands what was once the chapel or oratory of St. Winefride, where pilgrims were wont to spend the night in vigil before bathing. Unfortunately it is now in Protestant hands, and used for the Welsh services of the parish church; but the Well itself, the property of the corporation of Holywell, has for a considerable time been held at an annual rent by the Jesuit Fathers of the Mission.

...[The spring] water being very cold, never rising above 50 degrees Fahrenheit in any weather, and never freezing. Chemical analysis has never detected any mineral or medicinal properties peculiar to it, that would account for the extraordinary cures, which are often instantaneous. The overflow from the octagonal basin passes into a long narrow piscina, which is entered by steps at either end. Those seeking a cure pass through this piscina, reverently kneeling in the cold water and kissing an ancient cross carved in the stonework. The hard limestone steps are literally worn away by the bare feet of pilgrims. From this piscina the water passes under a low arch into a small swimming bath, with bathing cots on either side, and then flows onward through Greenfield Valley to join the River Dee .... In a corner opposite the entrance to the crypt where the spring rises, a statue of St. Winefride stands in a decorated niche. The pilgrims on emerging from the piscina throw themselves on their knees before this statue, earnestly imploring the saint's intercession.

The Latin Mass Society Pilgrimage

The LMS Pilgrimage has long been one of the most important of the Society's annual events, attracting hundreds of people each year.

It takes place customarily on the first Sunday of July. After High Mass in the Church of St Winefride, the Parish Church of Holywell which is close to the Shrine, the pilgrims process the short distance to the Holy Well, where they venerate a relic of St Winefride. They then return to the church for Benediction.

HYMNS IN HONOUR OF ST WINEFRIDE
FULL OF FAITH

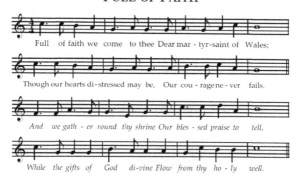

Full of faith we come to thee Dear mar-tyr-saint of Wales;
Though our hearts di-stressed may be, Our cou-rage ne-ver fails.
And we gath-er round thy shrine Our bles-sed praise to tell,
While the gifts of God di-vine Flow from thy ho-ly well.

We have come from far and near,
As pilgrims to thy feet;
We have brought our loved ones here,
Thy pity to entreat.

Thy sweet fame hath spread abroad
To lands beyond the sea,
And the children of the Lord
Bless God because of thee.

We have come to thank thee too,
Thy miracles to own;
Our glad promise to renew
To live for God alone.

Help us, sweet Winefride,
To love and suffer still,
Get us grace, whate'er betide,
To do God's holy will.

Oh, bring back the ancient faith!
Bring back the second spring!
Let thy mountains and thy heath
With loving 'Aves' ring!

Make us pure as thou wert pure,
As dauntless and as true;
Get us patience to endure,
Till heaven at least we view.

251

MORE FAIR THAN ALL THE VERNAL FLOWERS

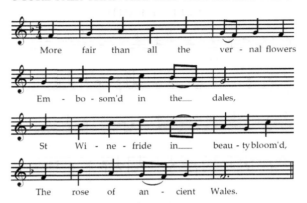

More fair than all the ver - nal flowers

Em - bo - som'd in the___ dales,

St Wi - ne - fride in___ beau - ty bloom'd,

The rose of an - cient Wales.

With every loveliest grace adorn'd,
The Lamb's unsullied bride,
Apart from all the world she dwelt
Upon this mountain side.

Caradoc then, with impious love,
Her fleeing steps pursued,
And in her sacred maiden blood
His cruel hands imbrued.

He straight the debt of vengeance paid,
Ingulf'd in yawning flame;
But God a deed of wonder work'd
To her immortal fame.

For where the grassy sward received
The martyr's sever'd head,
This holy fountain upward gush'd,
Of crystal vein'd with red.

Here miracles of might are wrought;
Here all diseases fly;
Here see the blind, and speak the dumb,
Who but in faith draw nigh.

Assist us, glorious Winefride,
Dear virgin, ever blest!
The passions of our hearts appease,
And lull each storm to rest.

Edward Caswell (1814-78) 252

LITANY IN HONOUR OF ST WINEFRIDE

Lord, have mercy on us.   *Christ have mercy on us*
Lord, have mercy on us.   *Christ have mercy on us*
Christ, hear us.   *Christ graciously hear us*

God, the Father of heaven,   *Have mercy on us (etc.)*
God, the Son, Redeemer of the world,
God, the Holy Ghost,
Holy Trinity, one God,

Holy Mary,   *Pray for us (etc.)*
Holy Mother of God,
Holy Virgin of virgins,

Saint Winefride,
Glorious virgin and martyr,
Faithful spouse of Christ,
Kind and loving virgin,
Sweet comforter of the afflicted,
Bright example of chastity,
Shining star,
Fair flower of ancient Wales,
Chosen vessel of grace,
Mirror of purity,
Mirror of devotion,
Mirror of piety,
Shining lamp of sanctity,
Hope of distressed pilgrims,
Patron saint of Holywell.

That we may be delivered from iniquity,   *Virgin and*
        Martyr, pray for us (etc.)
That we may be delivered from disordered passions of the
        mind,
That we may be delivered from deceits of the world, the
        flesh and the devil,
That we may be delivered from occasions of sin,
That we may be delivered from sickness, accident and
        sudden death,
That we may be delivered from the wrath of God and
        eternal damnation,
That we may have true sorrow for our sins,
That we may hate sin and overcome temptation,
That we may despise worldly vanity and delights,

That we may fear God and do His holy will,
That we may preserve chastity and purity of life,
That we may love humility and mildness,
That we may persevere in prayer and penance,
That we may bear our trials for the love of Christ,
That the souls in Purgatory may obtain eternal rest,
That those who are suffering may obtain the grace of
    patience and be comforted,
That God, in His mercy, may bless this pilgrimage,
That God, our Father, may grant our petitions,
That through thy gentle aid we may obtain health of mind
    and body,
That our Lady Mary may always protect us,
That we may be made worthy of the promises of Christ,

Prayer in Honour of St Winefride

Almighty and everlasting God, Who didst enrich St. Winefride with the gift of Virginity, grant us we beseech thee by her intercession to set aside the delights of the world, and to obtain with her the throne of everlasting glory.

Almighty and everlasting God, we humbly beseech thee, that St. Winefride may obtain for us such spiritual and temporal benefits as are expedient to Thy holy service and our eternal salvation.

O Blessed Winefride, pure virgin and glorious martyr, so especially chosen, so divinely graced and so wonderfully restored from death to life! Hope of all that fly unto thee with full confidence and humility! We, though unworthy, yet thy devoted pilgrims make our petitions unto thee (Pause), Sanctuary of piety, look upon us with patient eyes; receive our prayers, accept our offerings, and present our supplications at the throne of mercy, that through thy powerful intercession, God may be pleased to bless our pilgrimage, and to grant our requests and desires, through Christ our Lord. Amen.

(Glory be, x3)

PILGRIMAGE TO YORK

St Margaret Clitherow
(from the *Catholic Encyclopedia*).

Martyr, called the "Pearl of York", born about 1556; died 25 March 1586. She was a daughter of Thomas Middleton, Sheriff of York (1564-5), a wax-chandler; married John Clitherow, a wealthy butcher and a chamberlain of the city, in St. Martin's church, Coney St., 8 July, 1571, and lived in the Shambles, a street still unaltered. Converted to the Faith about three years later, she became most fervent, continually risking her life by harbouring and maintaining priests, was frequently imprisoned, sometimes for two years at a time, yet never daunted, and was a model of all virtues. Though her husband belonged to the Established Church, he had a brother a priest, and Margaret provided two chambers, one adjoining her house and a second in another part of the city, where she kept priests hidden and had Mass continually celebrated through the thick of the persecution. Some of her priests were martyred, and Margaret who desired the same grace above all things, used to make secret pilgrimages by night to York Tyburn to pray beneath the gibbet for this intention. Finally arrested on 10 March, 1586, she was committed to the castle. On 14 March, she was arraigned before Judges Clinch and Rhodes and several members of the Council of the North at the York assizes. Her indictment was that she had harboured priests, heard Mass, and the like; but she refused to plead, since the only witnesses against her would be her own little children and servants, whom she could not bear to involve in the guilt of her death. She was therefore condemned to the peine forte et dure, i.e. to be pressed to death. "God be thanked, I am not worthy of so good a death as this", she said. Although she was probably with child, this horrible sentence was carried out on Lady Day, 1586 (Good Friday according to New Style). She had endured an agony of fear the previous night, but was now calm, joyous, and smiling. She walked barefooted to the tollbooth on Ousebridge, for she had sent her hose and shoes to her daughter Anne, in token that she should follow in her steps. She had been tormented by the ministers and even now was urged to confess her crimes. "No, no, Mr. Sheriff, I die for the love of my Lord Jesu", she answered. She was laid on the ground, a sharp stone beneath her back, her hands stretched out in the form of a cross and bound to two posts. Then a door was placed upon her, which was weighted down till she was crushed to death. Her last words during an agony of fifteen minutes, were "Jesu! Jesu! Jesu! have mercy on me!" Her right hand is preserved at St. Mary's Convent, York, but the resting-place of her sacred body is not known. Her sons Henry and William became priests, and her daughter Anne a nun at St. Ursula's, Louvain.

[Note: St. Margaret Clitherow was canonized by Pope Paul VI in 1970.]

The Latin Mass Society Pilgrimage to York

St Margaret is one of the LMS' two Patron saints, with St Richard Gwyn. The Pilgrimage first took place in 2011. Customarily it takes place on the Saturday closest to the day of St Margaret's martyrdom, 25th March.

The Pilgrimage starts with Mass at the Church of St Wilfrid, which is close to York Minster. This is followed by a long procession through the streets of York, passing first St Margaret's house in the Shambles (a simple shrine to St Margaret has been set up in one of the nearby houses), and then the place of her execution on a bridge. The procession ends at the Church of the English Martyrs, where a relic of St Margaret is venerated, followed by Benediction.

In 2012 the pilgrimage was joined by Bishop Drainey of Middlesbrough.

PILGRIMAGE TO WREXHAM

St Richard Gwyn (from the *Catholic Encyclopedia*)
Martyr, born at Llanilloes, Montgomeryshire, about
1537; executed at Wrexham, Denbighshire, 15 October,
1584. After a brief stay at Oxford he studied at St.
John's College, Cambridge, till about 1562, when he became a schoolmaster, first at Overton in Flintshire, then
at Wrexham and other places, acquiring considerable reputation as a Welsh scholar. He had six children by
his wife Catherine, three of whom survived him. For a
time he conformed in religion, but was reconciled to
the Catholic Church at the first coming of
the seminary priests to Wales. Owing to his recusancy he
was arrested more than once, and in 1579 he was
a prisoner in Ruthin gaol, where he was offered liberty if
he would conform. In 1580 he was transferred
to Wrexham, where he suffered much persecution, being
forcibly carried to the Protestant service, and being frequently brought to the bar at different assizes to undergo
opprobrious treatment, but never obtaining his liberty. In
May, 1583, he was removed to the Council of the
Marches, and later in the year suffered torture
at Bewdley and Bridgenorth before being sent back to
Wrexham. There he lay a prisoner till the Au-
tumn Assizes, when he was brought to trial on 9 October,
and found guilty of treason and sentenced on the following day. Again his life was offered him on condition that
he acknowledge the queen as supreme head of
the Church. His wife consoled and encouraged him to the
last. Five carols and a funeral ode composed by
the martyr in Welsh have recently been discovered and
published.

[St Richard was canonised in 1970.]

The Latin Mass Society Pilgrimage
The Wrexham Cathedral houses the shrine of St Richard .
The pilgrimage, including veneration of the relic, takes
place on a Saturday near his feast day in October. St
Mary's Cathedral, Wrexham LL11 1RB , Wales.

PILGRIMAGE TO OXFORD

The Latin Mass Society's Pilgrimage to Oxford honours the five Catholic martyrs executed in the city: four of them in 1589, on the town gallows, and the fifth in 1610, on the Castle gallows.

The Martyrdoms of 1589

Bl George Nichols (from the *Catholic Encyclopaedia*)
English martyr, born at Oxford about 1550; executed at Oxford, 19 October, 1589. He entered Brasenose College in 1564 or 1565, and was readmitted 20 August, 1567, and supplicated for his B.A. degree in 1570-1. He subsequently became an usher at St. Paul's School, London. He arrived at Reims with Thomas Pilchard, 20 Nov., 1581; but went on to Rome, whence he returned 21 July, 1582. Ordained subdeacon and deacon at Laon (probably by Bishop Valentine Douglas, O.S.B.) in April, 1583, and priest at Reims (by Cardinal Archbishop Louis de Guise) 24 Sept., he was sent on the mission the same year. Having converted many, notably a convicted highwayman in Oxford Castle, he was arrested at the Catherine Wheel Inn, opposite the east end of St. Mary Magdalen's Church, Oxford [now part of Balliol College], together with Humphrey Prichard, a Welsh servant at the inn, Thomas Belson, and **Richard Yaxley.** This last was a son (probably the third...) of William Yaxley of Boston, Lincolnshire, ... Arriving at Reims 29 August, 1582, he received the tonsure and minor orders 23 Sept., 1583, and the subdiaconate 5 or 6 April, 1585, from the cardinal archbishop. Probably the same hand conferred the diaconate on 20 April. The priesthood was conferred at Reims by Louis de Breze, Bishop of Meaux, 21 Sept., 1585. Yaxley left Reims for England 28 January, 1585-86.

All four prisoners were sent from Oxford to the Bridewell prison in London, where the two priests were hanged up for five hours to make them betray their hosts, but without avail. Yaxley was sent to the Tower as a close prisoner 25

May, 1589, and appears to have been racked frequently. Belson was sent to the Gatehouse. The other two remained in Bridewell, Nichols being put into a deep dungeon full of venomous vermin. On 30 June all four were ordered back to Oxford to take their trial. All were condemned, the priests for treason, the laymen for felony. Nichols suffered first, then Yaxley, then Belson, and last Prichard. The priests' heads were set up on the castle, and their quarters on the four city gates.

Bl. Thomas Belson (from the *Catholic Encyclopaedia*)
Martyr, b. at Brill in Oxfordshire, England, dated uncertain; d. 5 July 1589. He was at the college in Reims in 1584, ... He suffered after the priests and, kissing the dead bodies of his pastors, begged the intercession of their happy souls that he might have the grace to imitate their courage and constancy.

The Martyrdom of 1610

Bl George Napier (or Napper) (from the *Catholic Encyclopaedia*).
English martyr, born at Holywell Manor, Oxford, 1550; executed at Oxford 9 November, 1610. He was a son of Edward Napper (d. in 1558), sometime Fellow of All Souls College, by Anne, his second wife, daughter of John Peto, of Chesterton, Warwickshire, and niece of William, Cardinal Peto. He entered Corpus Christi College 5 January, 1565-6, but was ejected in 1568 as a recusant. On 24 August, 1579, he paid a visit to the English College at Reims, and by December, 1580, he had been imprisoned. He was still in the Wood Street Counter, London, on 30 September, 1588; but was liberated in June, 1589, on acknowledging the royal supremacy. He entered the English College, Douai, in 1596, and was sent on the mission in 1603. He appears to have lived with his brother William at Holywell. He was arrested at Kirtlington, four miles from Woodstock, very early in the morning of 19 July, 1610, when he had on him a pyx containing two consecrated Hosts as well as a small reliquary. Brought before Sir Francis Eure at Upper Heyford (Wood

says before a justice named Chamberlain), he was strictly searched; but the constable found nothing but his breviary, his holy oils, and a needle case with thread and thimble. The next day he was sent to Oxford Castle, and indicted at the session soon after under 27 Eliz., c. 2 for being a priest. The possession of the oils was held to be conclusive and he was condemned, but reprieved. In gaol he reconciled a condemned felon named Falkner, and this was held to aggravate his crime, but as late as 2 November it was believed that he would have his sentence commuted to one of banishment. As he refused the oath of allegiance, which described the papal deposing power as a "false, damnable, and heretical" doctrine, it was decided to execute him. He suffered between one and two in the afternoon, having said Mass that morning. ... His quarters were placed on the four city gates, but at least some were secretly removed, and buried in the chapel (now a barn) of Sanford Manor, formerly a preceptory of Knights Templar.

The Latin Mass Society Pilgrimage

The Pilgrimage commenced in 2005, and begins with Solemn Mass in the Dominican Rite in The Priory Church of the Holy Spirit, in Blackfriars, in central Oxford, on the second Saturday of Michaelmas Term (usually the third Saturday of the month). After a break for lunch, the pilgrims gather for a procession to one or other of the sites of martyrdom, which usually alternate year by year. The martyrdoms of 1589 are marked by a slate plaque on 100 Holywell Street; the martyrdom of 1961 is marked by a steel plaque in the Oxford Castle complex.

After reaching the site of martyrdom, the procession returns to Blackfriars for Benediction.

In 2008 Bishop William Kenny blessed the newly installed plaque to the martyrs of 1589, in the presence of members of the family of one of the martyrs, Bl. Thomas Belson. In 2010 Archbishop Longley blessed the newly installed plaque in honour of Blessed George Napier.

OTHER PILGRIMAGES
OF THE LATIN MASS SOCIETY

Aylesford, Kent: in honour of Our Lady of Mount Carmel. The modern Carmelite complex, completed in 1965, incorporates the buildings of the medieval Carmelite community, which had become a private house; it is the national centre for the Brown Scapular. The pilgrimage takes place on a Saturday in October. Aylesford, Kent ME20 7BX.

Brinkburn, Northumbria: the Medieval Priory, of Augustinian Canons, was re-roofed in Victorian times and the Pilgrimage Mass takes place in it, on a Saturday in September. Brinkburn Priory, Longframlington, nr Morpeth NE65 8AR.

Caversham, Berkshire, in the outskirts of Reading: in honour of Our Lady of Caversham. The shrine, at the parish church of Our Lady and St Anne, is the restoration of an important Medieval shrine dating from before the Norman Conquest, and visited by Queen Catherine of Aragon. The Shrine image is a Medieval Virgin and Child from Germany, and it is housed in a fine chapel built in the Norman style. The present shrine was blessed in 1958; the shrine image was crowned in 1996. The pilgrimage takes place when possible on the Ember Saturday of Lent. Our Lady and St Anne, 2 South View Ave, Reading RG4 5AB.

Glastonbury, Somerset. Mass takes place in the parish church, and after a break for lunch there is Benediction and a rosary procession through the ruins of the Abbey. Bl Richard Whiting, the last Abbot of Glastonbury Abbey, was martyred on the Tor. Glastonbury was the most ancient monastic house in England, dating from before Saxon times; according to legend St Joseph of Arimathea planted his staff here: the Holy Thorn which grew from it is, against all the odds, still growing. The Pilgrimage takes place on a Saturday in September. St Mary's Church, Magdalene St, Glastonbury, Somerset, BA6 9EJ.

Padley, Derbyshire: in honour of the Padley Martyrs, the priests Bl Nicholas Garlick and Bl Robert Ludlam. Mgr Benson's 'Come Rack, Come Rope' is based on their story. They were captured in Padley Manor House and executed in Derby in 1588. The Manor's secret chapel, hidden in the upper floor of the gatehouse, was restored as a shrine in 1933; the original altar stone was found in the ruins of the Manor . The pilgrimage takes place on a Sunday in June. Access is via a track closed to visitors' cars, which starts by Grindleford Station (S32 2JA).

Tyburn, London, in honour of the English Martyrs. Pilgrims walk from the site of Newgate Prison where prisoners were held, to the site of the 'Tyburn Tree', the gallows where they were executed, following the martyrs' route down what is now Oxford Street, ending at the Tyburn Convent.

West Grinstead, Sussex: in honour of Our Lady of Consolation. The fine parish church of Our Lady of Consolation houses the first shrine to be established in England since the Reformation, in 1876; the image was also the first to be officially crowned, in 1893. It had been an important Catholic centre during Penal Times; the secret chapel in what is now the presbytery can be visited. Bl Francis Bell, who served the area, was a Fransiscan martyred in 1643. The churchyard contains the grave of Hilaire Belloc. The Pilgrimage usually takes place on a Saturday in May. West Grinstead, Horsham, West Sussex RH13 8LT.

Willesden, London: in honour of Our Lady of Willesden. An important Medieval shrine, visited frequently by St Thomas More, one of whose daughters lived nearby, it was restored in 1931. The shrine is in the parish church of Our Lady of Willesden, and the shrine image is made from a beam of the medieval shrine. It was crowned in 1954. In the 1950s and early 1960s it was visited by St Jose-Maria Escriva. The Pilgrimage takes place on a Saturday in June, with Mass, a break for lunch, followed by Benediction and other devotions. Our Lady of Willesden, 1 Nicoll Rd, London NW10 9AX.

INDEX OF LATIN CHANTS, HYMNS ETC..

INDEX OF ENGLISH HYMNS & SONGS

INDEX OF FRENCH HYMNS ETC.

Index of Prayers